How to Get

an

Cirencester College
Library

New Specification OCR H573/1,2,3

New edition

By Peter Baron

Published by Active Education

www.peped.org

First published in 2018

ISBN: 9781983346590

©Active Education Ltd

Cartoons used with permission © Becky Dyer

Exam Questions and Religious Studies specification H573 © OCR Exam Board

All images © their respective owners

Links, reviews, news and revision materials available on www.peped.org

With over 40,000 visitors a month, the philosophical investigations website allows students and teachers to explore Philosophy of Religion and Ethics through handouts, film clips, presentations, case studies, extracts, games and academic articles.

Pitched just right, and so much more than a text book, here is a place to engage with critical reflection whatever your level. Marked student essays are also posted.

Contents

Introduction to the New Specification

In 2016 the new specification introduced some fundamental changes to the OCR Religious Studies exam to bring it in line with Government requirements.

- There are now three papers, with the majority opting for Christian Thought H573/3 as the third paper. This has presented some challenges such as the introduction of four new areas of study: pluralism, secularism, feminism and liberation theology. The issue addressed here is - how do you integrate three papers so they make one coherent whole?

- The rationale for doing AS levels has changed. If you try to do the AS exam as a one year course you will find there is too much content to complete it in the time available. This is because it is designed as a two year course to be done as equivalent of half an A level. The prediction is that AS levels as a one year course will therefore disappear. Teachers have been slow to realise that AS is designed as a stand-alone two year course.

- The logic of doing an AS exam one year and then an A2 exam the next year has disappeared for another reason: you cannot count the AS mark towards your GCE A level qualification (it's no longer referred to as A2) – so some would say, why bother to do the exam? You have to take the whole GCE exam at one go.

- It follows that it is even more important to understand the detail of the specification and to give yourself the best chance to score well in the exam at the end of the second year. The pressure has

1

increased on gaining that A grade because the exam is meant to be harder, for three reasons:

1. You do three questions out of a choice of only four. The old specification required you to do only 2/4.

2. The questions set can be from any part of the specification - we can't assume two questions will be from Year 1 material and two from Year 2. Indeed the whole concept of a Year 1 and Year 2 part becomes fairly irrelevant and teachers would be wise to think through which components they do first, and which components they do in parallel with a second or even a third teacher.

3. There is a sixth level of GCE assessment (only five at AS level), so it may be true that it will be harder to achieve an A* (but let's wait and see on this point).

Notice also that the number of retakes is also predicted to soar – for people who just miss their preferred university by a grade or so. In the old system you could retake your AS level in January of your second year and then even a third time in May, and there was no need to declare that you'd done badly first (or second) time round. This is no longer possible. January retakes have now gone, and as mentioned above, you cannot count an AS towards an A2 full A level anyway. Basically, you now choose to do either an AS or a full GCE A level.

The specification is brief and fairly general. For example, there are relatively few authors mentioned and even those that are mentioned do not form a comprehensive list. This means that teachers and students have to make their own decision on how to interpret the specification. I am going to show you how I would tackle this paper in a later chapter – but for the time being please be aware that you should think carefully about the approach you wish to take.

Textbooks produce their own interpretation of the specification. There are two authorised (OCR validated) textbooks, one by Wilcockson and Wilkerson (Hodder 2017), and one by Ahluwahlia and Bowie (OUP, 2017). These books try to condense their own approach into a certain number of pages, inevitably – but this is not the only possible overview to adopt, and there is danger in this condensing activity. It can lead to over-simplification and the very unphilosophical approach to this subject of 'learning the textbook'. I will try and explain as we go through this specification in later chapters how you need to adopt a courageous approach to this exam, and develop your own ideas and pursue the authors that interest you – as the selection of authors and arguments considered by textbooks is not the only selection. We need to keep our eyes focused on the specification alone.

Let me sum this all up in five clear points, the points which teachers occasionally seem to be confused about.

1. The AS level is not supposed to be a step on the way to full A level but a stand-alone two year course, with five levels of assessment on full essays (but no part a and part b as with other boards).

2. The six levels of assessment at full GCE A level need to be carefully understood. They are designed to make the top grades harder to achieve - let's wait and see what happens.

3. The specification says we should cite 'scholarly views', but there's been a somewhat futile debate on how many scholars students should be citing in an essay. Read this book and I will try to explain why this is a rather meaningless question.

4. You have one attempt at this exam after two years. You need to build essay-writing skills carefully over this period. My chapter on what philosophy is about may help you here. There is some evidence that as the exam nears, students become cautious,

textbook-dependent and lapse into GCSE thinking, for example, believing that there is some magic formula for writing a good essay, such as PEREL, (which stands for Point, Explain, Response, Evaluate and Link). I'm not sure about this: there is no formula except writing philosophically, attacking the question in front of you, and understanding what this means.

5. Question-spotting for the forthcoming exam may be harder than with the old specification. But we need to pay close attention to the suggested areas, usually four, mentioned in the specification under each section with the phrase, "Learners should have the opportunity to discuss issues related to..." My chapter on Essay Questions analyses these and discusses what kind of question we might expect.

Five Principles for A level Success

In my previous book on the old specification I suggested five principles which will greatly enhance your A grade prospects which still hold good.

PRINCIPLE 1 - Understand the philosophy behind your exam.

PRINCIPLE 2 - Do a close analysis of the exam specification.

PRINCIPLE 3 - Do a close analysis of possible questions and 'trigger words'.

PRINCIPLE 4 - Do a close analysis of the relation between specification and questions.

PRINCIPLE 5 - Do a close analysis of the Chief Examiner's mark schemes, indicative content suggestions, and reports.

The main difference in my approach here is that we do not have many exam reports to analyse, and only some sample questions and one full set of GCE exam papers as guidance. I have included my chapter based on the exam reports on the previous specification as the points raised by examiners will essentially remain the same. After all, we are still studying the same subject.

I have also adopted a more radical approach and tried to imagine myself as the Chief Examiner, setting my own list of questions. Remember no exam question can be set twice (but some of the textbook examples might be set, as happened in 2018). Use this list throughout the course and make sure you can answer the questions I've created.

Finally, I include throughout the book some ideas on how to revise effectively, both as an individual and as a group, including a number of class revision exercises.

What Are Religious Studies Exams For?

Is there a reason for religious studies/philosophy exams, a philosophy behind the subject you are now doing?

The answer is "yes", and it helps if you understand the philosophy behind Philosophy, Ethics and Christian Thought, and see them as one integrated whole, because in the end, if you become a philosopher and can show this in the exam, you should gain close to full marks.

The word philosophy means "a love of wisdom", and we gain wisdom by exercising a special type of thinking skill. The Greeks believed this skill was a foundational skill, because thinking well was a key to living well. So, we might ask, how do we "think well"?

I was encouraged recently to hear of a school which has a cookie club which meets at 4pm every week on a Thursday. The idea of the cookie club is to meet and debate - or if you like, to argue a case. Sometimes a member of staff, and sometimes a pupil comes with a case to defend, and everyone has to argue against the point of view that pupil is defending.

Something like this underlies the subject of philosophy. Philosophy is about presenting, arguing and then defending a case. So for example, Plato uses a method of dispute in his writing, called the Socratic method, where he puts words into the mouth of an adversary and then proceeds to dispute and disprove that opponent's case.

Of course this begs some questions.

What Do I Actually Believe About, Say, Gay Marriage?

I awarded a prize a few years ago to anyone who could provide a good philosophical case against gay marriage (actually I'm in favour of gay marriage, this was just a philosophical exercise about understanding different points of view). I announced the prize at a conference, and I guess it was no surprise that the speaker next to me murmured "there isn't one".

The speaker is of course wrong. The problem is, we sometimes need moral courage to oppose a view which most people hold. If I (for the sake of argument) was to oppose gay marriage, some people might call me a homophobe, and other people may describe me as a right-wing fundamentalist, out of tune with reality.

But philosophers should not worry about this. Because philosophy is concerned with the nature and strength of arguments, and nothing else. People can cause me to take poison like Socrates had to, they can insult me in newspapers, and they can walk out of conferences. But we need to hold steadfastly to this point: social welfare only proceeds by the analysis and evaluation of arguments. It is only by this process that any great social reform has come. Bad arguments produce bad politics and bad policies and good arguments do the opposite. In your A level, have the courage to present, and then own for yourself, good, strong, well-justified arguments and you will be on the way to an A grade.

What Makes an Argument Weak?

A weak argument can really only be of two types. It can be logically unsound. We call this an error of deduction. And it can be factually unsound, or improbable. . We call this an error of induction. Some arguments may present both weaknesses.

For example, consider this argument:

1. The world is either flat or square.

2. The world is not flat.

3. So the world must be square.

What is wrong with this? Well, it is false in two senses. First it commits a logical mistake - of restricting the options. It only gives us a choice of two possibilities, flat or square, when in fact there are many possible shapes, and the correct answer, the world is round, isn't given as a possibility.

Secondly, it is empirically or factually false. As a matter of fact, if I set off in my little sailing boat and head west (assuming I remember to navigate for the Panama Canal) I will eventually end up where I started. So I can attack the argument on two grounds, the logical and the factual, making clear what my two grounds are.

What about this argument about euthanasia:

1. The command, 'thou shalt not kill' is absolute.

2. Elderly people, even those with poor quality of life, are still human beings.

3. Therefore you should never kill an elderly person.

What is wrong with this argument? It actually begs a question, or perhaps begs two questions. Is 'thou shalt not kill' absolute? After all, the Bible allows killing in times of war (Joshua 1-3) and also lists the death penalty for a number of crimes (Leviticus 18). So 'thou shalt not kill' (Exodus 20) cannot be absolute, but relative (conditional).

Secondly, the statement that 'you should not kill an elderly person' is emotive, designed to elicit the emotional response 'of course you shouldn't!'. But if we consider euthanasia no-one is arguing an elderly person should be allowed to die except with their consent, and if actively killed without consent, only in certain specific circumstances, such as in the case of Hillsborough victim Tony Bland who was found to be brain dead. So an answer to this question - should we allow killing in cases of euthanasia, really reduces down to issues about when, where, and in what circumstances, if any, it might be allowable or morally justifiable.

The word we use for this type of discussion is 'nuanced'. In other words, we need to avoid overstatement and over-generalisation and unpick the issues carefully. People are regularly allowed to die in the UK, which we call passive non-voluntary euthanasia, some of them tragically, children like Charlie Gard in 2017.

Some facts are important for ethics. So to argue 'ethics is about opinions not facts' is another false move. It is morally important where we can establish beyond doubt that the planet is warming and this is vital to business decisions about how to dispose of waste. It is morally important to know who suffers when the company Trafigura dumps toxic waste in the Ivory Coast, as it did in 2006, and how much compensation the inhabitants deserve for their suffering.

It is morally important whether someone in a persistent vegetative state (such as Tony Bland, a victim of the Hillsborough football stadium disaster in 1989 mentioned above) has any hope of recovery, and whether their brain still functions or has any hope of functioning normally.

But of course, we must check the facts. Bad facts produce bad ethics - and it wasn't long ago that some people were arguing that certain races were less intelligent than others, as a monstrous argument for discrimination, well considered in the 2013 film about President Lincoln. And both Aristotle and Aquinas set the cause of women's equality back centuries by arguing that women are less intelligent and less rational then men.

What Makes an Argument Strong?

A strong argument proceeds by a logical form, from assumptions to conclusion. On the way the argument requires analysis and, as the question at GCE level will demand it, evaluation. Many students don't understand the difference between analysis and evaluation, so perhaps we can clarify this.

Analysis means that an argument proceeds by a process of reasoning. When we reason we substantiate (back up) the argument. This means we give justifications for a particular viewpoint. For example, we say that Kant argues that morality is an a priori process of reasoning, because he sees the moral ought as applying universally, everywhere, and for all time, regardless of circumstances. If this is the case, then he argues we cannot base our decisions on emotions or peer group pressure, because this would make the moral ought conditional on what people think or what I feel at any particular time.

Notice that in this argument I use the word "because" a number of times. I spell out the reasons for my reasoning. I also use a hypothetical statement, which starts with if and then continues with then. The "if" here is indicating an underlying assumption, that we can divide the world up into two realms of thinking, what Kant calls the noumenal world (of pure ideas) and the phenomenal world (of experiences that we feel, see, touch).

If I was evaluating Kant rather than giving a Kantian analysis, then I might question this assumption. Is it a good way of looking at the world? Can there really be a pure realm of ideas in themselves? How do we know this world exists if it is completely inaccessible? Does this differ from the utilitarian view of the world, and is the utilitarian view superior? If so, why? If not, why not?

But notice that if the examiner is asking me just to explain the Kantian worldview then any evaluation is irrelevant. However, at GCE A level we are expected to evaluate as we go along, and so to discuss Kant's worldview and criticise it is certainly relevant.

In the new OCR specification you will only be asked to write full essays. Essays will always have both an analytic and an evaluative component – and you need to learn to weave the two together, and never, ever, just tack the evaluation on as an afterthought..

What Makes an Argument Interesting?

Believe it or not the examiner can get bored reading the same textbook-regurgitated material script after script. So we need to make our arguments interesting. There are two main ways of doing this.

Make your argument different

For example, where most candidates might be expected to approve of utilitarian ethics (as it's the dominant way of thinking ethically in our society), why not attack utilitarian ethics?

We could take as our starting point Arthur Koestler's quote, that people, in the name of utilitarianism, "have visited upon the human race such terrible privations..." and develop this idea.

Our development might go like this: Governments claim to be arbiters of the common good. In imposing a decision on society, they can, for utilitarian reasons, ignore dissenters and the rights of those who are adversely affected. They can justify this in the name of progress and general welfare. Which is exactly what totalitarian governments have done. You could then connect this idea to Stalin's forced collectivisation which led to the deaths of over ten million Russians.

Make your examples real

Examiners like us to use examples which are up-to-date or personal. In order to do this, we could use a film to illustrate our argument. Imagine we are talking about Kant's good will.

We could use the film Untouchable, which shows how an unemployed man caring for a disabled rich man in Paris would transform his life by relating to him as a human being with real needs and feelings, rather than as a category of "disabled". The carer in the film treats his sick employer as an 'end in themselves', as a real human being. In this way the care worker shows that goodness isn't about rules (how I should care for people) but about motives, and maxims such as 'be caring' and 'be truthful'

Or we could take an example from our own experience. Should we ever save a stranger in distress? Has anyone ever saved you, or have you ever saved a stranger? What is the moral motivation for doing so? Is it a feeling (which seems to argue against Kant) or a sense of duty (which seems to argue for Kant's idea that we act on duty alone)?

Or we might use books we are reading, novels, biographies or everyday descriptions from books. The point is, make our essays interesting and show we can relate abstract ethics and philosophy to real life, and we will make an A grade much more likely. That's one way of producing A grade reflection.

How Do I Practice Strengthening Arguments?

I have written another book called "How to Write Philosophy Essays" in this series. In that book I describe a technique for writing essays. Here's a brief description of how this technique works.

Imagine I have an essay title like "Miracles are unbelievable because they break natural laws", Discuss. I need to practise presenting what we can call my thesis in the first line of the essay. The thesis is simply your statement of your line of reasoning on this particular question. For example, my thesis might be "Miracles are believable because, although they may break natural laws, they do not have to do so; they may simply be unusual events, and even if they do break natural laws, they are miracles because they reflect who God is rather than human ideas of what is possible".

This statement has the advantages of being unmistakably relevant to this exact question and also very clear. The second thing I can do is reduce every paragraph to a one sentence statement of the argument of that paragraph.

THESIS - Miracles are believable because they depend on God's character not on human ideas of scientific possibility.

PARAGRAPH 1 - The biologist Richard Dawkins argues that nothing is possible outside of a scientific probability which is determined by our understanding of natural laws.

PARAGRAPH 2 - Many events are outside scientific understanding. Give examples.

PARAGRAPH 3 - The miraculous can mean one of two things - the improbable or the impossible. Quote some other authors (eg Swinburne).

PARAGRAPH 4 - The biblical account of miracles sees them as signs which point to the nature of God - as Creator (Jesus walks on water showing creator power), and redeemer (Jesus heals people with words like "Go in faith" and "Your sins are forgiven", so showing how to buy us back/redeem from death).

CONCLUSION - Judging miracles by scientific criteria is misguided as miracles should be judged against the probability or otherwise of the existence of God.

So, try to sketch out a thesis, practise this technique, and then try saying something interesting, surprising even, which of course must be fully justified. This is how you maximise chances of an A grade.

Why Do Definitions Matter So Much?

In Philosophy of Religion, Ethics and Christian Thought there is technical vocabulary which must be used correctly (see the appendix for a full list of the technical vocabulary in your course). But we need to be aware that the task of philosophy is also to indicate ambiguities in key words, how they are used differently in different contexts and how the meaning is not necessarily clear-cut or fixed.

The first A level (full GCE) paper in June 2018 had this question. "The best approach to understanding religious language is through the cataphatic way. Discuss." Now, the technical term 'cataphatic' is in the Philosophy of Religion specification under Religious Language which lists three elements:

- the apophatic way (via negativa)

- the cataphatic way (via positiva)

- symbol

Notwithstanding this, a very large number of students confused the cataphatic an apophatic ways. For this reason, I've included a glossary of all the technical terms in the new specification as an appendix, with a strong recommendation that you learn them off by heart.

I was listening to a debate on Question Time a few years ago and it became clear to me that two sides of this debate were actually talking about a different thing. The subject was gay marriage. On one side, the definition of marriage here meant something like "a relationship where two people are fully committed to one another". No mention of sexual relations here.

On the other side, the definition was something like this: "marriage is a lifelong commitment between a man and a woman where heterosexual sex is the natural expression, and children the natural fruit, of such a lifelong commitment". Notice that this definition includes both sex and the possibility of children.

I think the chairman of this debate, David Dimbleby, should have pointed out that people were talking about two different things. The question is, which is the correct definition, or the most useful definition? Clearly the second is the traditional view of marriage, whereby not having sexual relations is a ground for divorce or annulment of the marriage. Once we have established we are talking about different things we can then decide what we think.

Does it matter that the definition of marriage is changing? Should marriage necessarily include some idea of sexual relations if it doesn't, could I marry someone who remains my best friend, who I never even touch? If marriage includes some idea of sexual relations, how do we define sexual relations between two men?

All this helps to clarify the debate - and this is the task of philosophy. For philosophy has at its heart a philosophy of argument - of clarification, reasoning and conclusions which make sense. To argue effectively we cannot help defining and clarifying our terms, and indicating possible ambiguities in their use.

The examiner's reports, analysed in the final chapter, repeatedly emphasise a failure to grasp key terms is a major reason why candidates don't get A grades.

Four Integrating Principles in the Specification

The three papers may appear as fairly distinct strands of one religious studies rope. This may be misleading as a metaphor, however, because it is actually written as three thoroughly interlinked aspects of the study of religion and theology, which has always been a branch of philosophy. There is one rope, thoroughly intertwined. If we think more laterally, we find connections that go, as it were, sideways, and key thinkers such as Augustine or Aquinas appear in all three specifications either, implicitly or explicitly as named authors and thinkers.

Integrating Principle 1 - History

Ideas do not appear in a vacuum but emerge from stages of history, or world-views. These views are not static but go through stages of evolution, until a moment arrives for what Thomas Kuhn calls a 'paradigm shift'.

For example:

1. The Copernican Revolution of the fifteenth and sixteenth centuries saw a fundamental change of perspective as the world was no longer at the centre with the stars orbiting round it, but based on observation, the sun was established as the centre.

2. The Reformation which began with Martin Luther's nailing of ninety-five theses on the door of a church in Wittenberg in 1517 created an idea of the individual at the centre of our relationship with God, and the authority of the Church was thereby diminished.

Scripture and reason became paramount, but by elevating reason and the individual the Reformation also created an environment of thinking where human rights and equality came to the forefront of the agenda - in a sense sowing the seeds of religion's own demise.

3. Darwin's revolution, beginning with the publication of the Origin of Species in 1863, challenged theological understandings of the origin of the world and the uniqueness of humans. We were not God-created but naturally-evolved extensions of the animal kingdom. Darwinism is studied in the secularism section of the Christian Thought paper which considers Darwinism and Richard Dawkins' attack on religion and faith, but it is also relevant to the teleological arguments of thinkers like William Paley, who infer purpose from patterns and design. For Dawkins there is no purpose in nature.

4. Finally the psychological revolution, that began with Freud, fundamentally reinterprets what it means to be human, and the place of human responsibility and the concept of human sin. "Sin" becomes behaviour which we cannot accept according to prevailing norms, which are to be explained in terms of subconscious forces, such as repressed desires for a mother or father figure. Just as Freud interprets sin as socially unacceptable behaviour which can be explained by psychological drives, so the liberation theologians also fundamentally reinterpret sin as structural - coming from material facts of life, such as power relations reflected in property ownership and ownership of the means of production. Sin for a liberationist means unjust praxis.

Taking some of the key thinkers named by the specification and placing them into eras of history we can see the following stages are considered.

Era	Philosophy of Religion H573/1	Ethics H573/2	Christian Thought H573/3
Ancient	Plato, Aristotle	Aristotle	Plato, Arsitotle
Early Christian	Augustine, Irenaeus, Boethius		Augustine
Medieval	Anselm, Aquinas	Aquinas (Natural Law & Conscience)	Aquinas
Enlightenment	Kant Hume	Kant Utilitarians Hume	Calvin Kant Hume
Modern	Ayer Wittgenstein Malcolm Swinburne Hare Mitchell Hick	Fletcher Ayer Wittgenstein Freud (Conscience)	Hick (Pluralism) Dawkins (Secularism) Freud (Secularism)

The phrase 'paradigm shift' implies an instant revolution - but of course in practice new ideas take time (decades) to change the fundamental foundation world-view. Arguably we still live with vestiges of all world-views - for example, the fundamentalist version of Islam we find in the terrorist organisation ISIS is really a medieval mindset where death is visited on the idolater and blasphemer, the attitudes to women are barbarous, and the idea of the divine will and divine rewards primitive. It is exactly how Christians behaved to Muslims, and to each other, in the medieval period.

Notice also that something produces the shift and that arguably the big shift from the Greek worldview to the early Christian worldview is produced by the decisive entry of God into the world - in the incarnation of Jesus Christ - or at least, the influence of Christianity on the development of world-views is an important and foundational question.

It is interesting, though, to consider whether the Jesus movement was actually a Jewish reform movement or a radical break. The Jewish author Gaza Vermes has interesting insights into this question. Reversing this argument we can also see that John's gospel, written late in about AD90 is profoundly Greek in its ideas, with Jesus described as the Logos or divine word become flesh (John 1). Did Christianity influence philosophy, or philosophy influence Christianity? Feminist theologians such as Rosemary Ruether invoke the idea of Jesus as the genderless divine wisdom or Logos, showing a bias in favour of John's interpretation of the Christ-event.

Integrating Principle 2 - Hermeneutics

Hermeneutics means 'the study of interpretation' after Hermes who was messenger (interpreter) to the gods. The issue that underlies our specification is: how has the idea of God been interpreted over time and by different cultures? Does this explain the many varieties of Christianity we see in the world today, and the every different varieties in history - some very violent (the Crusaders), some pacifist (the Quakers), some quite radically prophetic (The Montanists), some world-renouncing (Monasticism), some ecologically friendly (Franciscans).

Hans-Georg Gadamer describes the 'two horizon's of hermeneutics. Professor Anthony Thiselton explains the metaphor of 'horizon' in this way:

The goal of biblical hermeneutics is to bring about an active and meaningful engagement between the interpreter and text, in such a way that the interpreter's own horizon is re-shaped and enlarged. In one sense it is possible to speak, with Gadamer, of the goal of hermeneutics as a "fusion" of horizons. In practice, because the interpreter cannot leap out of the historical tradition to which he belongs, the two horizons can never become totally identical; at best they remain separate but close. Nevertheless the problem of historical distance and tradition should not give rise to undue pessimism. Even if the problems of hermeneutics are not trivial, neither are they insoluble, and there is always progress towards a fusion of horizons. The Bible can and does speak today, in such a way as to correct, reshape, and enlarge the interpreter's own horizons. (The Two Horizons of Hermeneutics, page xix).

We tend to read the Bible and any ancient text from the perspective of our own time. In this way the Bible continues to live today in real applications. The liberation theologian shares with the feminist theologian a discerning of a golden thread of a prophetic-liberating tradition. Passages such as the Exodus are taken as describing the liberator God who intervenes to save his people from the appalling state of slavery in Egypt. The oppressors are judged by the miracle of the opening and closing of the waters, so that the pursuing armies of Pharaoh drown before they can attack the Israelites., swallowed up in a hell of water as the Red Sea closes in.

In a later chapter I consider how we should treat the passages which are listed in our specification (there are eleven in total and only two of these are from the Old Testament, Genesis 3 and Exodus 20). One excellent way to start the course in Year 1 is to examine carefully Genesis 3 and a New Testament parable such as Matthew 25, the parable of the sheep and the goats, first from a reader-response perspective (just read it raw and ask students to comment on the text and find resonances today, or in their own immediate experience) and then read the interpretations in history, for example, in Augustine or Aquinas or Calvin, or in modern times, from feminist and conservative evangelical.

Just seeing the variety of interpretations shows how Gadamer's task of fusing horizons is worked out in practice. In this process, try taking a radically new translation of the Bible such as The Message, which will help you really hear what it is saying. Familiarity breeds deafness when it comes to Bible stories.

Many of the debates in today's church (for example, in sexual ethics) are debates about hermeneutics and which principles we may or may not bring to bear in interpreting bible texts.

None of us, however, are entirely free from prejudice and preconception - and the claim to pure readings of Scripture made by different Christianities is really a form of power-play, saying in effect 'accept my interpretation, or you'll be damned', or in Roman Catholic terms, excommunicated. Of course, that is hardly the grounds for damnation given by Jesus in his parable of the sheep and the goats in Matthew 25 - which suggests that it's whether we treat the poor and the outcast as if treating Jesus himself that will be the grounds for division between saved and damned.

What you do to the least of these you do also to me, (Matthew 25:40)

Integrating Principle 3 - Metaphysics

Nietzsche (1844-1900) famously declared that "God is dead'. It may be truer to say God has been dying progressively since the Enlightenment project took hold, sparked by the Protestant revolution of the sixteenth century which, by enthroning the individual and human reason, opened a flood gate of autonomous reason and intellectual enquiry.

The British Social Attitudes survey of 2013 revealed that 51% of the UK population identified themselves as being of 'no religion', up from 31% in 1983. Research by sociologist Linda Woodhead has confirmed, however, that 'no religion' does not mean 'no belief in God'. Instead it seems to suggest a disillusionment with organised religion and a growing gap between what people generally believe about, say, gay marriage, and what the church teaches. The churches seem to lag behind popular culture in their attitudes on issues such as homosexuality, women's rights, contraception, abortion and euthanasia. Homosexuality and euthanasia are firmly on our specification (in the Ethics paper).

Linda Woodhead explains this tendency with reference to Peter Berger's work on secularism (see Christian Thought specification, section 5).

In order to explain the rise of British 'nones' it is still helpful, then, to begin with Peter Berger's old insight that cultural pluralisation is an important factor in religious change in modern societies. What he refers to in his latest book as the 'twin pluralisms' of (a) religious diversity and (b) religious/secular diversity are important factors in most parts of the world today, not least in the UK, a country which is now more religiously diverse than the USA. Berger places particular emphasis on the way in which pluralisation undermines taken-for-granted cognitive frameworks and traditions. In contexts of diversity it becomes harder and harder for religion to be an unquestioned part of the culture, handed down from generation to generation, as natural as the trees and the sky. (Linda Woodhead, Journal of the British Academy 4, 245–61, 2016).

She concludes that the major divide in Britain between the 'no religion' young and the greater religiously affiliated older population, is primarily based on a consensus amongst young people of 'tolerance, epistemological modesty and respect for the 'other'.

We study pluralism and secularism in the Christian Thought paper H573/3, but the shadows of these influences are cast over the other papers. Kantian ethics is an attempt to bring reason in a purer form to bear on ethics - his was a theory of the pure form because he fails to see how even his own categories of reason have to be tainted by cultural prejudice. This is the postmodern view that Woodhead describes as 'epistemological modesty' (meaning modesty about what we can claim to know for certain). Younger people often confuse this with the entirely different propositions that 'anything goes' or 'you're entitled to your opinion'. When challenged on this view, by asking for example whether genocide is simply a matter of opinion, they of course protest 'of course not'. Epistemological modesty can also mean epistemological incoherence. Being modest is not the same as being a pure relativist, as we can argue for shifting universals - absolutes such as the belief that the world now goes round the sun are based on sound propositions and research. Anything simply doesn't go.

In the postmodern era metaphysics hasn't died, despite the attempts by Enlightenment philosophers from David Hume to John Stuart Mill to Dawkins and Freud to kill metaphysics by explaining it as some error of logic or infantilism of the human psyche. There are two reasons why metaphysics (and so God) hasn't died. The first is the recognition that we do speak meaningfully about God and other metaphysical concepts such as beauty, truth and love, by using special language games (to employ Wittgenstein's term). Those who inhabit these 'forms of life' also understand the shared game of language that is being played. It is a realm of symbol, metaphor, allegory, poetry. It's a form of philosophical totalitarianism to declare these games out pf play.

Secondly, authors such as Freud and Dawkins (see secularism part of the Christian Thought specification, or Freud on conscience in the ethics specification), fail to recognise their own metaphysical preconceptions. You cannot prove empirically (verify) Freud's categories of id, ego, and superego. They are metaphysical tools of explanation that allow his theory to progress. They may or may not be useful, but that is a utilitarian question. They are metaphysical nonetheless, and as much a 'fiduciary framework' or framework of faith as a Catholic or Protestant Christian worldview (which of course are not necessarily identical).

Finally consider Richard Dawkins, author of The God Delusion. It's good to study his views as they have become mainstream as part of the general lack of acceptance of many of the core beliefs of Christianity (such as the interpretation of women as less rational than men, held by most denominations of Christianity until the twentieth century). Dawkins argues for a selfish gene which is an evolved altruistic gene (so not morally selfish at all) that instinctively requires us to save a drowning child. Apparently it is a gene, but on examining our genes under a microscope we will never find one gene saying to another 'after you'. It is a metaphysical assumption or hypothesis that underlies Dawkins' work - a best fit explanation for human behaviour imposed on genetics (which is a science). The Enlightenment protagonist is simply a metaphysician in disguise, beguiling us with stories in order to fulfil an agenda to debunk God.

So our third integrating principle is this: we are examining the place of metaphysics in human experience and the unsuccessful attempt by the Enlightenment project to discredit metaphysics.

Integrating Principle 4 - What Does it Mean to be Human?

There have been seismic shifts in our understanding of what it means to be human from the times of ancient Israel, through the Greek philosophical worldview, the time of Jesus, Augustine, Aquinas, Calvin, and Kant and Hume, and in modern times, Freud and Dawkins.

If we keep this question to the forefront of our minds, we can trace the influences of different movements in the three papers. The question underlies all three papers, because even when we are considering arguments (for example) for the existence of God (Philosophy of

Religion) it is God-in-relation-to-human beings which we are considering.

Ancient Israel defined humanity by two contradictory ideas. We were made in the image of God, male and female, and so profoundly equal (Genesis 1) and yet by the purity code of the Old Testament book of Leviticus we are also defined as profoundly unequal as menstruating women were excluded from the Temple, and women generally excluded from the inner sanctuary. In other words, gradations of humanity are apparent in the Old Testament, defining different levels of holiness or cleanness. The themes of clean and unclean resonate through the Bible and so by Jesus time it seems Jesus could not accept some of these aspects of what is called the holiness or purity (cleanness) code of Leviticus.

Was Jesus a radical prophet of liberation overturning the codes just as certainly as he overturned the tables of the money-changers in the Temple (Mark 11, Matthew 21, John 2:13-16)? We can read him as such, as the liberation theologians do (see the Christian Thought paper on Liberation Theology). How can this radical and angry Christ of the Temple be reconciled with the sweet, blonde, effeminate Christ of Holman Hunt's Light of the World (the painting which hangs in St Paul's Cathedral)? Is to be human to be defined biologically (so male and female are unequal, as Aristotle taught, 'females are deformed males'), or theologically, as Paul implies when he says 'the male was formed first', and so is superior? Or is the gender difference to be defined as Augustine does, with reference to sin - and the temptation of Eve - as Eve seduces Adam and releases original sin to the world? We see the origins of the polar opposites of the myths of the dangerous whore (Mary Magdalene) and the pure virgin (Mary the mother of Jesus), which feminist theologians are so critical of.

There is a fundamental division here between Catholic and Protestant views of the human person. The Catholic view is that male and female are made in the image of God, and so human beings are endowed with reason and fundamentally good (follow through the discussion of synderesis in Aquinas for the full force of this argument, as synderesis means that every human being has a tendency to pursue good ends given by an innate conscience or sense of right and wrong).

The Protestant view following the Reformation has been that human beings are sold into sin and need to be redeemed or ransomed back from a slavery to sin by the Cross. We appropriate this salvation by a personal response of faith. Following Augustine, the Reformers stress an original sin that marks us all. Taken to extremes this means we cannot see God at all without grace. God reaches down to us to unblind our eyes. The Barth/Brunner debate which is mentioned in the suggested reading in the Christian Thought, Knowledge of God section, echoes again with this age-old debate about what it means to be human; are we fundamentally good or bad? Notice in ethics how free individual choice begins to take hold of ethical theories in the utilitarianism of Mill or the a priori rationalism of Kant. Kant requires autonomy as a postulate because if humans cannot self-legislate, literally make the moral law for ourselves how can we be moral at all?

Finally the twin paradigm shifts mentioned in Integrating Principle 1, that of Darwinism and Freud in the nineteenth century, fundamentally altered our view of what it means to be human, and not always to the good. For the Darwinist, humans are genetically-evolved animals with superior mental faculties sharpened by millennia of survival strategies that include co-operation. Yet we are still animals. We have no soul (whatever that word means). There is no need for God to explain the presence of our higher intelligence. The downside is that this sounds like a form of genetic determinism. We are our genes and they are pre-programmed. Remember that in Nazi Germany those who had 'unworthwhile lives' were deemed unworthy of life, and killed (the mentally 'subnormal' for example) until Bishop Galen thundered against it from his pulpit in Munster, in a famous and brave sermon in 1941. His words are telling:

According to the information I have received it is planned in the course of this week to move a large number of inmates of the provincial hospital at Marienthal, classified as "unproductive members of the national community," to the mental hospital at Eichberg, where, they are to be killed with intent. Since such action is not only contrary to the divine and the natural moral law but under article 211 of the German Penal Code ranks as murder and attracts the death penalty, I hereby report the matter in accordance with my obligation under article 139 of the Penal Code and request that steps should at once be taken to protect the patients concerned by proceedings against the authorities planning their removal and murder, and that I may be informed of the action taken. (Bishop Galen, sermon preached in Munster, 1941).

Before we feel morally superior, recall that in the USA the state of Indiana imposed forced sterilisation on 'imbeciles and mentally subnormals' in legislation dated 1907. Over 30 states followed suit, continuing the practice in some cases up until the 1960s. Over 65,000 individuals were forcibly sterilised in 33 American states. To be human meant a higher form of rational human. Those who didn't fit this definition of genetic purity were not allowed to have children. The Levitical purity code reinvented itself in genetics and eugenics and became an ugly deformation of our understanding of what it means to be fully human.

How crucial, then to keep this question to the forefront of our minds - what does it mean to be human, and in what ways are sections of our own society, or nations of our world, being dehumanised even as I write this?

How to Analyse the Specification

Students can sometimes be surprised by questions set in the exam. However, there never should be any element of surprise, as the specifications (syllabuses) lay down exactly what you can expect in the exam. Therefore surprise can only come because there is an area of the specification we failed to notice, or failed to cover adequately. A grade technique involves:

- Examining the specification, paying close attention to specific authors mentioned.

- Relating past questions to the specification to see how the examiner interprets the specification, which may be ambiguous in places.

In this section we will analyse the specifications for the papers Philosophy of Religion, Ethics and Religious Thought, before matching the specification to possible future questions in a later chapter.

Philosophy of Religion (OCR H573/1)

There are six syllabus areas and the first three are taken for an AS qualification and all six for a full GCE A level. Here are the six areas with the named major thinkers in brackets.

1.1 Ancient Philosophical Influences (Plato and Aristotle)

1.2 Soul, Mind and Body (Plato, Aristotle, Descartes)

2.1 Arguments for the Existence of God - Observation (Aquinas, Paley, Hume)

31

Interpreting the Philosophy Specification

Philosophy is about the understanding and evaluation of world-views with their hidden assumptions and ways of looking at things. It's a vital task because we all inhabit a worldview but have difficulty seeing how it imposes values and perceptions on us and so this connects with two of my integrating principles in an earlier chapter: the history of thought and hermeneutics. A worldview is like a pair of sunglasses that are heavily tinted with a certain colour. If I put on my blue-tinted Ray-bans the world looks different from the perception given by my pink-tinted lenses.

This section introduces us to two world-views that are fundamentally different but which find their echoes throughout history (this is synoptic point which we are encouraged to make – synoptic meaning 'bringing two things together for comparison').

Plato's view is that reality exists beyond the senses in world of the Forms – a set of pure forms of being which sum up the essence of reality (hence the form of a table expresses the essential nature of a table). Plato's worldview is very similar to the view of Immanuel Kant which we study in the Ethics paper. Kant called the 'forms' 'noumenal categories' and argued they could not be accessed directly by experience.

The Aristotelean worldview is very different. Aristotle argued that the only reality that exists is the one directly accessed by our senses – Aristotle was an empiricist (meaning he believed everything needed to be confirmed and tested by the five senses).

So the way to understand how to get beneath this section of the specification is to take the examiner's hint very seriously and get underneath the skin of two very different world-views – **Platonic rationalism** versus **Aristotelean empiricism** – and to compare them, and feel the essential difference between them.

Then we can find echoes of these two world-views in other areas of the course and indeed, in our own culture, and make allusions to these to gain synoptic credit.

Technical Vocabulary

There are 37 technical words or phrases which must be throughly understood as they may well appear in exam questions, and anyway, need to be mastered to use in essays. They are defined in the glossary of terms at the back of the book, where brief guidance as to why they are relevant.

A posteriori

A priori

Analogy of attribution

Analogy of proper proportion

Attributes (divine)

Category error

Cognitive approaches to language

Cosmological

Efficient cause

Empiricism

Fall

Fallacy

Falsificationism

Five Ways

Formal cause

Material cause

Materialism

Metaphysics

Mystical experience

Natural Religion

Nature of attributes of God

Non-cognitive approaches to language

Omnibenevolence

Omnipotence

Omniscience

Ontological

Prime Mover

Rationalism

Soul

Substance dualism

Teleological

Teleology

The Forms

Theodicies

Verificationism

Via negativa (anaphatic way)

Via positiva (cataphatic way)

Named Theologians and Philosophers

We are concentrating on the names in the specification itself, under each section, and then adding a column for suggested reading (which are suggestions of further philosophers and theologians, but only recommendations). It is up to you who you actually refer to in your essay, as long as it is relevant to your argument. There are many other philosophers and theologians in the world, and you may find the study of different ones to either the recommendations here, or indeed, the textbooks.

Section	Named	Suggested
Ancient Philosophical Influences	Plato and Aristotle	Plato, *Republic* Book 474c–480; 506b–509c; 509d–511e; 514a–517c Aristotle, *Physics* II.3 and *Metaphysics* V.2 Annas, J. *An Introduction to Plato's Republic,* Oxford University Press, Chapters 9 and 10 Stanford Encyclopedia of Philosophy, *Plato*
Soul, Mind, Body	Plato, Aristotle, Descartes	Descartes, *Principles of Philosophy,* I.60–65 Blackmore, S. *Consciousness; an introduction,* Routledge, Chapters 1, 2 and 17 Ryle, G. *The Concept of Mind,* Chapter 1 Stanford Encyclopedia of Philosophy*Ancient Theories of the Soul*
Arguments based on observation	Aquinas, Paley, Hume	Aquinas, *Summa Theologiae*, I.2.3 Paley, *Natural Theology* Chapters 1 and 2 Hume, *Dialogues Concerning Natural Religion* Part II Aquinas, *Summa Theologiae*, I.2.3 Paley, *Natural Theology Chapters 1 and 2* Hume, *Dialogues Concerning Natural Religion* Part II
Arguments based on reason	Anselm, Gaunilo, Kant	Anselm, *Proslogion* 2 & 3 Gaunilo, *In behalf of the fool* Kant, *A critique of pure reason,* Second Division III.IV Psalm 14.1 Van Inwagen, P. 'Necessary Being: the Ontological Argument' in Stump, E and Murray, M. J. *Philosophy of Religion: The Big Questions,* Blackwell Plantinga, A. *God, Freedom and Evil,* Grand Rapids, II.c

Religious Experience	William James	James, W. *The Varieties of Religious Experience,* lectures 9,10,16,17 and 20 Acts 9.4–8, 22.6–10, 26 Otto, R. (1923/1968) *The Idea of the Holy,* Oxford University Press, Chapters 4 and 5 Saint Teresa of Avila, from *The Autobiography of Saint Teresa* (1960/2010) Allison Peers, E. (ed. and trans.)
Problem of Evil	Augustine, Hick	Augustine, *The City of God* Part II Hick, J. *Evil and the God of Love,* Part IV Genesis 2:4–25, 3:1–24 Romans 5:12–13 Augustine, 'What is evil?' in Davies, B. *Philosophy of Religion: a guide and anthology,*
Nature or attributes of God	Anselm, Boethius	Boethius, *Consolation of Philosophy,* Book V Anselm, *De Concordia* Swinburne, R. *the Coherence of Theism,* Part II Matthew 19:23–26 Vardy, P. (1999) *The Puzzle of God,* Harper Collins, Section 4 Macquarrie, J. (1966) *Principles of Christian Theology,* SCM Press, Chapter 11
Religious Language - ancient	Aquinas, Tillich	Aquinas, *Summa Theologiae* I.13 Tillich, *Dynamics of Faith,* Part 3 Ayer, A. J. (2001) *Language, Truth and Logic,* Dover Publications Swinburne, R. (1997) 'God-talk is not evidently nonsense' in Davies, B. (2000) *Philosophy of Religion: a guide and anthology,* Oxford University Press Internet Encyclopedia of Philosophy, *Religious Language*
Religious Language C20th	Ayer, Hare, Flew, Mitchell	Ayer, A. J. *God Talk is Evidently Nonsense* Wittgenstein, L. *Philosophical Investigations* Swinburne, R. (1993) *The Coherence of Theism,* Oxford University Press, Part I Internet Encyclopedia of Philosophy, *Religious Language*

There are nineteen names, but as there are a number of repetitions, we find seventeen philosophers or theologians. There is a huge overlap between the specification for religious language and meta-ethics, which is why teachers often take them together. Two very useful reference sources are the Stanford Encyclopaedia of Philosophy and the Internet Encyclopaedia of Philosophy - both get two mentions each under suggested reading. Of the two, Stanford is definitely harder and needs to be used selectively. You will find the figures of Augustine and Aquinas loom large over all three specifications (Aquinas for example, appears in Natural Law ethics as one of its prime advocates, and in Christian Thought, Augustine is there in human nature, the first section).

Aquinas could be a source in Christian Thought for Natural Theology. Both Aquinas and Augustine are also targets for feminist theologians for their representation of an order of creation in natural law which places women lower than men (as less rational).

Synoptic Links in Philosophy of Religion

- Plato – Gender and Theology in Christian Thought. Greek philosophers argue for the lower rationality of women.

- Plato – Natural and Revealed Theology of God. Plato implies that during birth/reincarnation we still have a sense of the forms, hence children have a sense of right and wrong. Natural Law also argues that we are born with a sense of the Divine hence all civilisations have a sense of a higher power (Cicero). Calvin's sensus divinitatis, Latin for 'sense of the divine'.

- Aristotle – Cosmological Argument. Aristotle talks about how everything remains in a constant state of motion, from potentiality to actuality; similar to the Design qua Regularity argument.

- Aristotle – Problem of Evil. In both sculptor analogies apply, from Aristotle and from Irenaeus. Human potentiality to be Godlike and actuality is being human, and so limited.

- Aristotle – Cosmological Argument. 'Nothing comes from nothing' and the uncaused causer element are very similar ideas.

- Teleological Argument – links to Natural and Revealed Theology of God in Christian Thought. Can we deduce God exists from what we see in nature?

- Teleological Argument – Problem of Evil. David Hume's criticism of the teleological argument, that a good God wouldn't create a world with so much suffering. All we can infer is 'an infant deity'.

- Teleological Argument – Problem of Evil. Dawkins' digger wasp example links to Secularism and the God Delusion in Christian Thought.

- Teleological Argument – Natural and Revealed Theology of God. Links to Natural law in Ethics as Aquinas' term for conscience, synderesis, is a moral sense which we have innately, by design.

- Body Mind and Soul – Plato links with Death and the Afterlife in Christian Thought. There must be a permanent afterlife because of logic of opposites, says Plato. If our world isn't permanent then there must be another one that is.

- Problem of Evil – Aquinas; theory of Natural Law in Ethics implies human nature is fundamentally good as we're made in God's image.

- Problem of Evil – Teleological Argument. Use Dawkins' digger wasp example as argument against God's benevolence.

- Problem of Evil – Teleological Argument. David Hume's criticisms of the Teleological argument: a good God wouldn't create a world with this much suffering.

- Religious Experience – Pluralism and Society. in Christian Thought Interesting to link Feuerbach and Kraemer's arguments that most religions are cultural constructs.

- Religious Experience – link to Freud's Future of an Illusion in Christian Thought, and ideas of religion as neurosis, projection and a form of infantilism.

- Attributes of God – Christian Moral Principles. in Christian Thought Bible-Believing Christians argue there are many times where God appears to be interacting with humans in time e.g Genesis. Should these stories be taken literally? What about Joshua's slaughter of innocent people in Jericho in the book of Joshua?

- Attributes of God – Death and the Afterlife. Divine Foreknowledge supports the idea of limited election from Calvin in Christian Thought paper.

- Religious Language – Ontological Argument/Cosmological Argument. Discussion of analytic and synthetic statements applies to both.

- Religious Language – Religious Experience. Symbolic language arguably evokes numinous experiences.

Ethics (OCR H573/2)

The introduction to the course describes the aims of religious ethics:

"Religion and ethics is characterised by the study of ethical language and thought, with exploration of key concepts and the works of influential thinkers. Ethical theory will also be applied to issues of importance; namely euthanasia, business ethics, and sexual ethics".

The specification begins with normative ethics - the theories of natural law, situation ethics, Kantian ethics and utilitarianism, then picks up two applied ethical areas - business ethics and euthanasia. The fourth section turn to meta-ethics (ethical language) and then two further sections address conscience and sexual ethics.

Technical Language in the Syllabus

As we read through these specifications some general points seem to stand out. The first is that the specification helpfully breaks each topic up into subheadings. The second is that these subheadings contain specific technical language. The examiner has listed the technical language which, as a minimum, we are expected to use, and which we might expect to appear in the questions set.

So what is the technical language? You could take this opportunity to tick off the ones you can define easily without looking up.

Technical language in the Ethics specification includes forty-one terms:

absolutism

act utilitarianism

agape

categorical imperative

conscientia

corporate social responsibility

divine law

ego

emotivism

eternal law

extramarital sex

formula of kingdom of ends

formula of law of nature (law)

formula of the end in itself (ends)

globalisation

hedonic calculus

hypothetical imperative

id

intuitionism

invincible ignorance

meta-ethics

natural law

naturalism

personalism

positivism

postulates

pragmatism

primary precept

ratio

relativism

rule utilitarianism

sanctity of life

secondary precept

stakeholders

superego

synderesis

telos

utility

vincible ignorance

whistle-blowing

working principles

Now this is a minimum list (see the appendix for precise definitions) - there are more technical terms we might want to use in an essay that the specification doesn't mention - but we should start with this list and make sure we understand exactly what these terms mean and indeed, what the alternative interpretations of their meanings might be.

For example, the term sanctity of life in the Euthanasia section has a different meaning to a situation ethicist than it does to a Roman Catholic natural law theorist. To a situation ethicist , it means rejecting the Kantian maxim, "never treating a human being as just a means to an end", and as Fletcher makes it clear 'the end always justifies the means' and so rejects this absolutist Kantian view.

To Fletcher anyone and anything goes if we can establish that action maximises love. Of course, this begs the question of whether the embryo should be classed as a human being. But to a Roman Catholic, sanctity of life means "designed and created by God with absolute value" which includes embryonic life, as life begins at conception and must be protected.

Authors Mentioned

The following authors are mentioned, and although the syllabus makes clear you are not expected to read original sources, I believe the A grade candidate will want to read these authors for themselves. Extracts are available on the peped website in the relevant section. There are no specific authors mentioned for the applied ethics side of the specification: a good student will however draw up their own list of authors who address issues raised by the specification.

Section	Specification names	Suggested Reading names
1. Natural Law	Aquinas	Aristotle Physics II 3 Catechism 1954-1960
2. Situation ethics	Fletcher	CS Lewis Four Loves ch6 N. Messer Christian Ethics ch1
3. Kantian Ethics	Kant	L.Pojman Discovering Right and Wrong ch8 O.O'Neill in Ethical Theory: an Anthology
4. Utilitarianism	None	Bentham, J. *An Introduction to the Principles of Morals and Legislation* Mill, J.S. *Utilitarianism* Singer, P. *Practical Ethics*, Cambridge: Cambridge University Press Pojman, L. *Discovering Right and Wrong*, Stamford: Wadsworth, Chapter 7
5. Euthanasia	None (but see natural law and situation ethics sections which remain relevant)	Glover, J. *Causing Death and Saving Life*, London: Penguin Books, Chapters 14 and 15 Sacred Congregation for the Doctrine of the Faith (5th May 1980) *Declaration on Euthanasia* Singer, P. *Rethinking Life and Death: The Collapse of our Traditional Ethics*, Chapter 7
6. Business Ethics	None (but see Kant and utilitarian sections which remain relevant)	Friedmann, M. (September 13, 1970) 'The Social Responsibility of Business is to Increase its Profits', in *The New York Times Magazine*, The New York Times Company Crane, A. & Matten, D. (2003) *Business Ethics*, Oxford: OUP
7. Meta-ethics	None	Moore, G.E. (1903) *Principia Ethica*, Chapter II Ayer, A.J. (1936) *Language, Truth and Logic*, London: Victor Gollancz, Chapter 6 Mackie, J.L. (1977) *Ethics: Inventing Right and Wrong*, London: Penguin Books, Part 1.3

8. Conscience	Freud Aquinas	Fromm, E. (1947) *Man for Himself: An Inquiry into the Psychology of Ethics* London: Routledge, IV.2 *Internet Encyclopaedia of Philosophy, Sigmund Freud,* http://www.iep.utm.edu/freud/ Strohm, P. (2011) *Conscience: A Very Short Introduction,* Oxford University Press, Chapters 1 and 3
9. Sexual Ethics	None (but see all ethical theories which are still relevant)	Pope Paul VI (1968) *Humanae Vitae* Church of England House of Bishops (1991) *Issues in Human Sexuality,* London: Church House Publishing Mill, J.S. (1859) *On Liberty,* Chapter 1

The above analysis produces a startling fact: only five authors/philosophers are named in the Ethics specification H573/2. Under utilitarianism no philosophers are named at all, but fairly obviously the specification requires us to know about Bentham (who invented the idea of the hedonic calculus for calculating the pleasure of an action, which is listed as a piece of technical language) and Mill (who didn't invent the term rule utilitarianism, but was classified in 1953 by JO Urmson as a weak rule utilitarian).

Any of these five authors might be named in an exam question - so be warned.

Where scholars and texts are stated in the "Key Knowledge" or "Content" sections it is expected that learners would have sufficient knowledge of these to answer a question directly referencing them. (OCR Specification 2016).

However, the specification also requires us to

a. Understand the levels of response grids, discussed in a later chapter. The Levels of Response grids, used for assessment, credit learners for use of:

"Scholarly views, academic approaches and sources of wisdom and authority to support their arguments. Learners will be given credit for referring to any appropriate scholarly views, academic approaches and sources of wisdom and authority, not only those suggested in the specification document". (OCR Specification H573, page 6).

b. Understand synoptic links. Section 3f of the assessment criteria states (my underlining for emphasis):

"Synoptic assessment targets learners' understanding of the connections between different elements of the subject. Synoptic assessment is present in all A Level components, as they draw together both of the distinct assessment objectives in OCR's A Level in Religious Studies. It is also present due to the nature of the content and questions for all components. Learners can respond to questions in a variety of ways, using a wide range of possible material from across topics and components. All legitimate approaches and interpretations will be credited." (OCR Specification H573 page 101) .

From the above analysis we can conclude three important things:

1. You are expected to cite scholarly views, but the syllabus is entirely open-ended about whom you cite, naming only five authors directly.

2. The suggested reading is for advice only - but the advice should not be ignored. I have posted summaries (or in some cases, such as the Catholic Catechism, direct sources) of all of these suggested readings on the peped website.

3. The authorised textbooks have many more named authors. Yet, be clear, the textbook writers have simply given you their

interpretation of the specification. Arguably they have introduced too many new authors - as it's the quality of analysis that matters and your serious engagement with range of scholarly views that matters for an A* answer.

There is a big danger that students will be encouraged to machine-gun names at the exam question, without producing evidence of proper engagement with authors or weaving a critical analysis. Discussions with the OCR board have verified that you don't even need to name an author to engage with their viewpoint, although you're probably wise to do so.

The brave teacher may decide not to use the textbooks at all, or use them very sparingly, and provide their own, more limited but more in depth analyses of scholarly views that bring the specification, with its bare-bones approach to naming anyone, much more to life.

At the GCE level we are required (unlike some specifications, such as AQA) to do a full blooded analysis-evaluation as one sustained argument. OCR is surely correct to present a syllabus that aims at cultivating this higher-order skill.

I would suggest two ways of preparing for this critical-thinking skill inherent in the syllabus.

When we look at each theory, it is important to ask what the starting point or assumptions are, and to do this.

Secondly, we need to understand the worldview which the philosopher is coming from. In the table below I summarise how assumptions and worldview interact in the major ethical theories which we encounter at AS and GCE A level Ethics.

THEORY	ASSUMPTIONS	OBJECTIONS
Natural law	Humans by nature do good	Humans by nature are selfish and do more evil than good
Kantian ethics	Reason is divided between the noumenal and phenomenal realms, and morality belongs to the noumenal.	Moral principles seem to be derived by many philosophers from the natural or empirical world eg by adding up happiness.
Utilitarianism - Bentham	Pleasure is the only good. We can measure pleasure.	There seem to be other "goods" such as duty. We can't measure pleasure in hedons or anything else.
Situation ethics	there is one supreme moral principle - agape love and this is a realistic goal to live by	Agape is one of the four loves of Greek ethics and is the highest moral principle as it means repeatedly sacrificing yourself for a stranger. Possibly impossible to live by.
Utilitarianism - Mill	There are higher and lower pleasures Rules are needed to maximise utility	This is a difficult distinction to make without sounding snobbish. Rules imply universal application - so when can you break them?

To sum up, I think we should only draw up tables of strengths and weaknesses, at least for the ethical theories in question, if we realise this is a way of analysing weaknesses in arguments or assumptions. Make sure you link counteracting views with a philosopher and preferably, a quote from a philosopher. Learn some of these evaluative quotes for the exam, as they give you ideas which you can develop in the substance of your own essays. The extracts in each section (listed as Extract 1, Extract 2 etc) are also presented in each section on the website to help you extract key quotes and ideas from philosophers both dead and alive, so that your essays can gain more weight and a sense of engagement with ideas.

Why Meta-Ethics?

Meta-ethics forms the first part of the Year 2 course (assuming we take topics chronologically in order of sections, which of course we needn't do) is the study of theories of ethical meaning and the foundations of ethics (the naturalism debate). This produces difficulties because of the technical vocabulary (see list above) such as emotivism and intuitionism, which have their own special implications. Why are theories of the meaning of good are actually required at all in this course?

Many philosophers would argue that meta-ethics is foundational to the subject as, remembering the discussion of the word marriage above, if we don't know exactly what we are talking about when we use the word "good" then we can find ourselves talking past one another. In fact today we live in an era of the resurgence of ethical naturalism, the view that ethical ideas have grounding in features of the natural world. This movement is led by philosophers like the virtue ethicist Alasdair MacIntyre, who wholeheartedly rejects the so-called naturalistic fallacy, and sees ethics grounded in a common idea of welfare derived from both the Bible and science. Of our ethical theories in the table on page 49, all except Kantian ethics are forms of naturalism. Can they all be wrong?

The second area of difficulty comes with the introduction of business ethics into the syllabus. Teachers have been unsure how to handle this topic. Again, there is technical vocabulary to learn (such as 'stakeholders') and some clarification to pursue as to how to use an idea like globalisation productively in an essay on ethics. My suggestion is to study business ethics through case studies such as Enron (2003) Trafigura (2009) or Ford Pinto (1973).

Critical Discussion

The GCE Ethics syllabus has left student and teacher with work to do filling in the gaps and interpreting how much additional content to supply. However, we can be reasonably certain that the examiner wants us to contrast different views and then to decide, with justifications, which view we side with. This seems to be implicit in the command words "Discuss" or "Evaluate".

One way to prepare for the exam is to decide beforehand what your conclusion would be for any question the examiner might ask. For example, if we are asked to evaluate emotivism or intuitionism it helps to have decided beforehand which theory we would side with, and why. What are the strengths and weaknesses of each? It is poor exam preparation to go into a paper unsure of your basic position.

So imagine we have the classic question "Goodness is merely an expression of personal feelings", Discuss. Underlying this question is the argument for or against emotivism. Suppose that we have decided that we quite like emotivism as a theory and thus wish to defend this assertion (whilst also considering objections to it of course).

I would then pre-prepare the following case: "Emotivism is the best explanation of the meaning of goodness because it recognises that the core element in statements of right and wrong is not reason, but

51

feeling, and that no naturalistic explanation of the meaning of goodness escapes the naturalistic fallacy". I can then research some other authors, extract some quotes and make my own summary sheet around this base position - which could be adapted for another question such as "intuitionism is the best theory of the meaning of goodness", Discuss, which you could then disagree with using the same justification of emotivism as a counter-argument.

Similarly, with business ethics we need to map out the territory clearly. Business ethics is only linked to two theories: Kantian ethics and Utilitarianism. So the range of questions is limited. In 2018 they asked:

"Kantian ethics is the best approach to issues surrounding business ethics". (OCR Ethics H573/2 2018)

This requires us to do two things - contrast Kantian ethics with some other theory (utilitarianism) and also to identify the 'issues surrounding business' which could include the issues of globalisation (exploitation if cheap labour for example) or issues surrounding the conflict between stakeholders who have different interests (the community versus shareholders, for instance).

Where there is inadequate structure in a specification, we must impose our own map to make sense of it.

Synoptic Links

Here is a list of synoptic links within the Ethics specification - links with other sections within this Ethics paper or links to themes in the other two papers. The more we can see such links, the more coherent this specification will feel and the better nuanced will be our essays.

- Natural Law – Situation Ethics. Both are forms of Christian ethic even though Joseph Fletcher eventually lost his Christian faith and was inspired by Marx.

- Natural Law – Natural and Revealed Theology of God in Christian Thought. Supports the idea that we can learn and understand God by using our reason and logic, instead of just using scripture.

- Natural Law – Heavily inspired by Aristotle particularly his idea of natural rational purpose, the four causes, and his use of empirical senses, so link to Philosophy of Religion, section on Aristotle.

- Natural Law – Natural and Revealed Theology of God. Four tiers of law shows scripture is one of two ways God reveals his eternal law - arguably superior and clearer than natural law. Even theologians like Aquinas who believe in natural law suggest it isn't as significant as direct revelation from God.

- Natural Law – Sexual Ethics. Humanae Vitae, 1968, suggests that due to the primary precepts or rational goals stemming from our created natures, marriage must remain solely for reproductive purposes.

- Situation Ethics – Person of Jesus/Christian Moral Principles, links with Christian Thought topics. Study Parable of Good Samaritan as a situationist parable about agape love, the individual and the context of a particular situation.

- Situation Ethics – Conscience. Fletcher's ideas of conscience as an active, doing verb, rather than a faculty of intuition as in Aquinas' synderesis, links with Daly's argument that God is a verb in the Gender and Theology section of Christian Thought.

- Utilitarianism – Liberation Theology. Bentham and Mill's "Greatest happiness for the Greatest number" has echoes in Marxist idea of the general good which could potentially be linked to Liberation Theology in Christian Thought.

- Utilitarianism – links to Liberation Theology. Utilitarianism can work against minorities or individuals, whereas the underside, the oppressed and the poor are 'preferred' in Liberation theology.

- Utilitarianism – Aristotle. The moral goal of happiness as that which should be sought as telos seems similar to the Aritotelean idea that the ultimate human telos is eudaimonia/happiness.

- Kantian Ethics – psychology/ theories of knowledge. Could use arguments about how we learn behaviour by watching other authorities do the same thing, this would undermine Kant's postulate of autonomy and argument for primacy of duty backed by autonomy (freedom to choose). Is behaviour due to authority's conditioning?

- Kantian Ethics – Meta-ethics. Kant stresses that in order to follow duty we must be free from emotion but is this possible? Emotivism follows Hume, who argues 'reason is the slave of the passions'.

- Euthanasia – Natural Law. Plenty of links and arguments about the Primary Precepts and what happens when two moral goods conflict. Aquinas' primary precepts were conceived in an age without the pressing issue of euthanasia e.g preservation of life in conflict with quality of life.

- Euthanasia – Situation Ethics. Argues that if love is better served by going against human rules or laws then that is moral – interesting as active euthanasia is still illegal in UK, but passive euthanasia isn't. Fletcher served as the President of the Euthanasia Society of America between 1974 and 1976.

- Business Ethics – Utilitarianism. "Greatest happiness for the Greatest number" poses an interesting question as it's debatable whether the stakeholders/shareholders or the customers are truly the greatest number. Also could be argued that due to globalisation, wealth is concentrated in the hands of a few large businesses rather then allowing happiness and wealth creation for local companies. This fundamental inequality violates utilitarian principles such as Bentham's 'everyone to count as one, and no-one as more than one'.

- Business Ethics – Kantian Ethics. It could be argued that Kantian Ethics doesn't support whistle-blowing as stresses the importance of promise keeping. Also plenty of 'not just means to an end' arguments to be made with sweat shops. cheap labour and using advertising to influence consumers to gain profit.

- Conscience – Natural Law. Synderesis and the use of recto ratio are fundamental to Natural Law. Ethics specification concentrates on contrasting Aquinas and Freud. Freud's Future of an Illusion is a set reference in Secularism (Christian Thought).

- Conscience – Situation Ethics. Both Aquinas and Fletcher seem to suggest that conscience is an act of doing something - for Aquinas conscientia is 'reason working through situations'.

- Conscience – Pluralism and society/theology. The idea of vincible and invincible ignorance has echoes in Karl Rahner's anonymous Christians who seek to do good and exhibit a moral sense .

- Conscience – Psychology. Bring in extra knowledge about psychological theories such as behaviourism to the answer if relevant.

- Conscience – Meta-Ethics. Kant claims that emotions have no part in true moral decisions, however emotivism suggests moral statements are simply expressions of emotion.Aquinas suggests conscience is a form of intuition implanted by God.

- Meta-ethics – Natural Law. Ethical Naturalism infuses Natural Law as both suggest that we can know about God and/or morals by observing the world around us and using reason.

- Meta-ethics – Utilitarianism. G.E Moore criticises utilitarianism as goodness isn't something that can be empirically quantified, but is simply known through an intuitive perception. Intuitionism argues that all of our ethical decisions should be based on our intuitions as moral decisions are indefinable ,yet self-evident.

- Meta-ethics – Natural Law. W.D Ross's intuitionism and Prima Facie Duties seem like a similar notion to the Primary Precepts from Natural Law which are also always right, and so absolute. NB W.D. Ross is not named on the specification, but why not use him?

- Meta-ethics – Ontological Argument or any topic with analytic/ synthetic statements discussed. A.J Ayer develops Hume's definition of analytic/synthetic statements, by adding that moral statements are neither, and so meaningless.

- Sexual Ethics – Natural Law. Very good link to the natural law primary precept of reproduction especially considering the influence of the Catholic Church in Latin America. Link to liberation theology and paradox that poor sexual health affects poor women more than men.

- Sexual Ethics – Secularism. When debating how the church could potentially be seen as a cause for social problems such as criminalising homosexuality, remember there are many aspects of the church which are consistently changing to become more accepting. Does this mean they lose sight of their original Christian message, and that Christianity dies a 'death of a thousand qualifications'. Are there any absolutes in sexual behaviour?

- Sexual Ethics – Situation Ethics. Bring in Joseph Fletcher's examples of ethical sexual situations e.g the POW camp pregnancy.

- Sexual Ethics – Kantian Ethics. The first two formulations, universalisability and the ends formulae can be used, Freedom/ autonomy is also a key postulate of Kant, so consent is needed.

- Sexual Ethics – Utilitarianism. Mill's Harm Principle can be used here. Also Mill was an avid supporter of women's rights and gender equality).

Christian Thought OCR H573/3

The Christian Thought paper is a development of the Christian Theology paper which featured as an option in the previous OCR specification (see Christian Theology by Michael Wilcockson for a useful introduction, much of which is still valid in the new specification). It has generated its own challenges for four reasons:

- It ranges widely both across history and across theology.

- It seems at first glance to lack an integrating principle.

- It seems to impose a very limited selection of thinkers (Augustine on human nature and Calvin on natural and revealed theology, for example)

- The sheer breadth of knowledge required by teachers is very challenging - even when huge areas such as liberation theology and feminist theology are narrowed down, yet still (apparently) `the exclusion of transgender theology is offensive', wrote one teacher on facebook recently!).

However, the first glance is actually deceptive.

If we adopt one of the integrating principles mentioned in an earlier chapter, such as hermeneutics or the history of thought, then a uniting theme emerges. As we move from enlightenment ways of thinking (Ayer's emotivism in meta-ethics and verificationism in religious language, for example), to the post-modern categories of Wittgenstein (language-games, forms of life), then the specification becomes 'a study of how interpretation of God and Religion alters during the Enlightenment and post-modern periods, and the effects of such changes on religious belief'. Such an integrating principle allows us to understand how our own experience of reality is filtered by categories and values imposed upon us by popular culture and approaches to education itself. Remember that our ultimate aim is to learn to read our own culture by understanding how the Enlightenment project forced metaphysics to the sidelines (the same metaphysics which is now reemerging, I would argue, all around us in new spiritualities and new concerns for metaphysical concepts of beauty, truth and love).

The selection of thinkers is narrow, this is true. But it allows us in building an evaluative sense to introduce people that particularly interest us (and failing that, which we consider might be interesting to our students). If we wish to introduce transgender theology when studying feminism, then why not, or virtue ethics (which rather regrettably was in the old OCR specification, but dropped off the new one) when considering Kant - these are both highly relevant.

The breadth of knowledge teachers require is challenging. The difficulty has been made much greater by the way the two validated textbooks handle the open-endedness of the specification by adding layers of additional authors. It has resulted in a futile debate about how many philosophers you should be mentioning in a forty minute essay. It's a futile question because you can get an A* by mentioning no-one at all, as the specification clearly states 'a wide range of **scholarly views** and opinions', not 'a wide range of scholars'.

The problem of the complexity of textbooks compared with the simplicity of the specification itself, can be illustrated, for example, by the Knowledge of God section of the Christian Thought paper. This mentions no specific thinkers at all, yet the Wilkinson and Wilcockson textbook introduces us to Calvin's Institutes (admittedly there in the 'suggested reading' section of the specification), before inviting us to consider such complexities as Alfred North Whitehead's Process Theology (a big subject in its own right). At the same time, the textbook fails to mention the new natural theology of Alister McGrath, arguably a much more interesting and more straightforward contrast to the Calvinistic line (should you decide to run with Calvin).

If we interpret the specification in terms that I have suggested here, as a study of how changes and shifts in interpretative frameworks (Enlightenment, Darwinist, Freudian) alter everything, including the way God is perceived and believed, then surely it is more profitable to contrast McGrath's post-modern natural theology with one from the Enlightenment era, before we then re-connect McGrath with Augustine (as McGrath claims he is rehabilitating Augustine's trinitarian natural theology). This is more coherent and a lot more straightforward.

As well as using the peped website, you might consult the excellent online resource philosopherkings.co.uk written by a teacher whose school did the old Christian Theology paper.

Named Authors

Which authors are named by the Christian Thought specification, and so required reading, and which are simply suggested reading, and so optional in Christian Thought?

Specification	Named	Suggested Reading
1. Augustine & Human Nature	Augustine Genesis 3	City of God, Book 14, Chapters 16–26 Confessions, Book 8 Chapman, G. Catechism of the Catholic Church paras. 385–409 McGrath, A.Christian Theology, Wiley-Blackwell, pages 348–355, 371–372 Romans 7:15–20
2. Death & Afterlife	The Sheep and the Goats' (Matthew 25:31–46)	Chapman, G. Catechism of the Catholic Church paras. 356–368, 1020–1050 Hick, J. Death and Eternal Life, Palgrave Macmillan, Part III McGrath, A. A Theology: the Basics, Blackwell, Chapter 8 Revelation 20: 2–6, 7–15 and 21:1–8
3. Knowledge of God	None	Romans 1:18–21 Calvin, J. Institutes of the Christian Religion I.I and I.II Acts 17:16–34

4.Person of Christ	Son of God in Mark 6:47–52 and John 9:1–41 Teacher of Wisdom in Matthew 5:17–48 and Luke 15:11–32 Jesus as Liberator in Mark 5:24–34 and Luke 10:25–37	McGrath, A. Theology: the Basics, Blackwell, Chapter 4 Theissen, G. The Shadow of the Galilean, SCM Press Chapman, G. Catechism of the Catholic Church paras. 422–478
5. Christian Moral Principles	None	Exodus 20:1–17 1 Corinthians 13:1–7 Messer, N. (2006) SCM Study Guide to Christian Ethics, SCM Press
6. Christian Moral Action	Bonhoeffer	Letters and Papers from Prison and The Cost of Discipleship, Chapter 1 Romans 13:1–7 Barmen Declaration (www.sacred-texts.com/chr/barmen.htm) Luke 10:38–42
7. Pluralism and Theology	None	Hick, J. (1995) God and the Universe of Faiths, SCM Press, Chapters 1 and 10 McGrath, A. (2010 5th Edition) A Christian Theology, Wiley-Blackwell, Chapter 17 D'Costa, G. (2009) Christianity and World Religions, Wiley-Blackwell, Chapter 5

8. Pluralism and Society	Catholic Church: Redemptoris Missio 55–57 Church of England: Sharing the Gospel of Salvation	The Doctrine Commission of the Church of England (1995) The Mystery of Salvation Church House Publishing, Chapter 7 Ford, D. The Future of Christian Theology, Wiley-Blackwell, Chapter 7 Pope Paul VI Nostra Aetate; Declaration on the relation of the Church to non-Christian religions
9. Liberation & Marx	Marx	Boff, L. and Boff, C. Introducing Liberation Theology, Burns and Oates Gutierrez, G. A Theology of Liberation, SCM Press, Chapter 4 • Congregation of the Doctrine of the Faith Instruction on Certain Aspects of the 'Theology of Liberation' • Wilcockson, M. Christian Theology, Hodder Education, Chapter 7
10. Gender & Society	Ephesians 5:22–33 Mulieris Dignitatem 18–19	Tong, R. Feminist Thought, Routledge, Chapter 1 McGrath, A.) A Christian Theology, Wiley-Blackwell, pages 88–89, 336–337 Messer, N. SCM Study Guide to Christian Ethics, SCM Press, Chapter 8. Ephesians 5:21–33

11. Gender & Theology	Ruether Daly	Radford Ruether, R. Sexism and God-Talk, Chapter 9 Daly, M. Beyond God the Father, Chapter 4 The Doctrine Commission of the Church of England The Mystery of Salvation Church House Publishing, Chapter 7 Ford, D. The Future of Christian Theology, Wiley-Blackwell, Chapter 7 Pope Paul VI Nostra Aetate; Declaration on the relation of the Church to non-Christian religions
12. Secularism	Freud Dawkins	Freud, S. The Future of an Illusion Dawkins, R. The God Delusion, Chapter 9 Ford, D. The Future of Christian Theology, Wiley-Blackwell, Chapters 3 and 6 British Humanist Society, https:// humanism.org.uk/ Dawson, C. 'The Challenge of Secularism' in Catholic World, also online http:// www.catholiceducation.org/en/ education/catholic-contributions/ the-challenge-of-secularism.html

The above table suggests there are just seven authors named. But notice, crucially, that there are nine passages from the Old or New Testaments. This means that a Bible passage could appear in an exam question, for example, "The Bible is sexist. Discuss with reference to Ephesians 5:22-33".

The suggested reading is just that - suggestions. But I have put up on the peped website either summaries of these readings, or where appropriate, the reading itself. I have also written introductory handouts for each section which provide my own selection of additional reading and exploration of what I consider to be the main sub-issues. I will discuss further how we handle any question with a Bible passage mentioned in them in the chapter on Possible Future Exam Questions. Again, there is a big question of hermeneutics around how we handle selected passages, and we need to do so carefully and with academic rigour if we're not to descend into GCSE platitudes on these key named texts.

Technical Vocabulary in Christian Thought

The following is a list of twenty-one technical terms mentioned in the specification which need to be thoroughly learnt and mastered. This compares with thirty-seven for Philosophy of Religion and forty-two for ethics. A full glossary of these terms and those in the other two papers is included as an appendix to this book.

Although there are fewer technical terms to learn for this paper, there are many more bible references mentioned by the specification, eleven Bible passages are required reading. This produces its own problems: how do you interpret one short passage from the Bible without understanding its context and the Jewish context in first century Palestine? We are back to the issue of hermeneutics (interpretation) mentioned in the earlier chapter here on integrating principles.

If we are to avoid a naive, GCSE style response to these passages we must interpret them with some care and diligence. I will mention more about the correct way to interpret Scripture on the chapter on possible future exam questions as questions which involve these passages and which name them are clearly valid to set for the exam itself. Here is the complete list of Bible passages we are required to throughly understand and master (specification section in brackets includes eleven passages), and also, the Bible passages mentioned in suggested reading, a further seven passages. All except two in **bold** are New Testament.

Genesis 3 (Augustine and Human Nature)

Matthew 25: 31-46 Parable of the Sheep and the Goats (Death and the Afterlife)

Revelation 20:2-6, 7-15 and 21:1-8 (suggested reading, Death and the Afterlife)

Romans 1:18-21 (suggested reading, Knowledge of God)

Acts 17: 16-34 (suggested reading, Knowledge of God)

Mark 6: 47-52 (Person of Christ, authority)

John 9:1-41 (Person of Christ, authority)

Matthew 5:17-48 (Person of Christ, moral teaching)

Luke 15:11-32 (Person of Christ, moral teaching)

Mark 5:24-34 (Person of Christ, liberator)

Luke 10:25-37 (Person of Christ, liberator)

Exodus 20:1-17 (Christian Moral Principles)

1 Corinthians 13:1-7 (Christian Moral Principles)

Romans 13:1-7 (suggested reading, Christian Moral Action)

Luke 10:38-42 (suggested reading, Christian Moral Action)

Ephesians 5:22-33 (Gender and Society)

Luke 24:9-12 (suggested reading, Gender and Theology)

Acts 16:13-15 (suggested reading, Gender and Theology)

Below is the full list of technical terms in Christian Thought. Remember these terms can appear without explanation in an exam question and are also the kind of terms the examiner expects you to sue in your essays.

agape (both a core principle of situation ethics and issue in the section on Christian Moral Principles)

exclusivism

fall

grace

inclusivism

innate

limited election

messiah

natural knowledge

normative means of salvation

original sin

pluralism

purgatory

repentance

salvation

secularism

sinful

son of god

summum bonum

universalist belief

unlimited election

Christian Thought - Underlying Issues

The main subdivisions of the Christian Thought paper are as follows (I have added the big questions that underly each section in order to introduce the discussion which follows on bringing the sections together):

1. Augustine and Human Nature

Q. What does it mean to be human? Are we inherently good or bad?

2. Death and the Afterlife

Q. What is the place of metaphysics in human experience, and especially the belief in, or possibility of a metaphysical afterlife?

3. Knowledge of God

Q. How do we 'know' anything metaphysical, ie beyond observation?

4. Christian Moral Principles

Q. Do we need God in order to know goodness and behave morally?

5. Christian Moral Action.

Q. What do heroes of the faith like Bonhoeffer (martyred in 1945), or Archbishop Romero of El Salvador (martyred 1980) teach us about the motive and outcomes of Christian moral behaviour?

6. Pluralism, Theology and Society

Q. How do we handle diversity and does it mean we're all relativists today?

6. Liberation Theology and Marx

Q. How have Marxist insights and context of extreme poverty changed the way we look at Christ? Is this a judgement on western rich Christians?

7.   Secularism

Q. How have the Darwinist and Freudian revolutions changed the way we view God and practise religion?

8. Gender, Society and Theology

Q. How has the rise of feminism affected both society and religion?

Let's consider in a moment how these different elements are integrated with the two other papers, Philosophy of Religion and Ethics. But notice first how there is a big liberating theme that cuts across a number of sections:

- Bonhoeffer (Christian Moral Action) was struggling against the horrendous oppression of Nazism (just as the Lutheran churches of Germany compromised with Hitler). It led him to the radical conclusion that Hitler had to be killed.

- Rosemary Ruether is a feminist liberation theologian (Gender and Theology) arguing that the Augustinian tradition of the Fall (Human Nature section) has led to a developing tradition in Christianity of the inferiority/irrationality/danger of women, which needs to be countered by rediscovering the golden thread of a prophetic/ liberating tradition in the Bible.

- Freud and Dawkins argue that Christianity infantilises human beings; Freud, because we project onto God our images of a Father figure who answers our needs and ameliorates our anxieties, and Dawkins, because the introduction of God stops us thinking and reacting to scientific discoveries, such as evolutionary biology. We need to be liberated in how we think.

- Liberation theologians, emerging in Latin America in the 1960s, challenge the church to stop being part of a corrupt and oppressive system which keeps the poor enslaved by poverty. Paradoxically, liberation theologians (like Guiterrez) often argue that feminist liberation is inappropriate to Latin America. There may be connections, but it's interesting that liberation theologians and feminist liberationists part company here, and in the theology of God. Ruether wants a genderless idea of God as Wisdom, whereas Guiterrez is quite happy with the male, freedom-fighter Christ.

All sections are asking us to pose a fundamental question - why has Christianity so often lagged behind movements in popular culture, and why has it so often simply reflected the oppressive class system, racism or political self-interest of its time?

Has Christianity been rumbled as another form of relativism, hiding behind veils of absolutist authority (such as appeal to the Word of God, or the claims of the Pope?). Is it a force for good, or a collaborator in evil?

Synoptic Elements

We now consider how the three papers cohere into one perfectly cogent unity; we can observe the following major synoptic links in the table below. remember we will be credited for making synoptic links in our essays, even thought the syllabus itself doesn't make them for us (they are implicit, rather than explicitly stated). In the table below, column 1 gives us the specification's general objectives, and then the next three papers give us themes from the three papers that meet these objectives.

Content	Christian Thought	P of R	Ethics
1. Religious beliefs, values and teachings in their interconnectio ns and as they vary historically and in the contemporary world, including all the following:	"Foundations", "Insight" and "Living" sections of specification		NL ethics as interpreted and developed by RC church, evangelical objections to NL Linked to teleological arguments & Dawkins' criticisms
a) the nature and existence of God, gods or ultimate reality	Foundations: Knowledge of God's Existence	Attributes of God A priori 'proofs' (ontological) and a posteriori (teleological and cosmological) arguments	Kant's postulates of God and Immortality and NL idea of eternal law
b) the role of the community of believers	Living: Christian Moral Principles, Christian Moral Action (Bonhoeffer links to situation ethics)		NL ethics as Roman Catholic Moral theology Situation ethics as Chrisiian relativism
c) key moral principles	Living: Christian Moral Principles, Christian Moral Action		Kantian Ethics Situation Ethics NL Ethics

d) beliefs about the self	Insight: Augustine on Human Nature	Teleological (Design) Argument	Conscience Aquinas and Freud
e) beliefs about death and afterlife	Insight: Death and the Afterlife		Kant's immortality postulate
f) beliefs about meaning and purpose of life	Insight: Augustine on Human Nature, Death and the Afterlife		NL telos Utilitarian Happiness
2. Sources of wisdom and authority including, as appropriate: (at least one of the following)	"Foundations" section of specification		
a) scripture and/or sacred texts and how they are used and treated	Living: Christian Moral Principles		RC Catechism as justification for NL ethics (Romans 2)
b) key religious figures and/or teachers and their teachings	Foundations: The Person of Jesus Christ		
3. Practices that shape and express religious identity, including the diversity of practice within a tradition	Living: Christian Moral Principles		NL RC Theology Situationist Liberal theology (Divine Command Evangelical theology)

4. Significant social and historical developments in theology or religious thought including all the following:	Spread throughout A Level material; as detailed below		Role of Enlightenment in ethical theory – rejection of NL and metaphysics, rise of Utilitarianism and Relativism
a) secularisation	Challenges: The Challenge of Secularism	Hume's attacks on teleological and cosmological arguments. Kant's attack on moral argument.	JS Mill as example of atheistic mindset
b) science	Challenges: The challenge of secularism (5)	Platonic idealism versus Aristotelean empiricism. Also reflected in different roles of natural theology (proof versus 'fiduciary framework').	Empirical worldview (Hume) influences Utilitarianism and Emotivism – critiques of naturalism Kant echoes Plato in view of noumenal forms
6. Two themes related to the relationship between religion and society, these may include:	Covered in "Society" or "Challenges" specification section		

73

a) the relationship between religious and other forms of identity			Joseph Fletcher and relativism debate. Supports atheistic humanist view of euthanasia.
b) religion, equality and discrimination	Society: Gender and Society	Religious Language – feminist critiques. Aristotle's justification of slavery.	NL justifications of racism and hierarchy eg US Civil War
c) religious freedom	Challenges: The Challenge of Secularisation	Religious experience as one form of universal sense of numinous.	Kant's autonomy postulate. Utilitarian equality precondition. Freudian attack on religion (conscience section)
d) the political and social influence of religious institutions			Freud Future of an Illusion (conscience) Rise of liberal situationism in Christian ethics (US Episcopal Church). RC and C of E approaches to euthanasia debate.

e) religious tolerance, respect and recognition and the ways that religious traditions view other religions and non-religious worldviews and their truth claims	Development: Pluralism and Theology, Pluralism and Society. New natural theology of Alister McGrath (postmodern).	Religious Language – language games relative to forms of life (Wittgenstein).	Meta-ethics and Wittgenstein's critique. Religion as one of many 'forms of life'. Objections to NL absolutism.
7. how developments in beliefs and practices have, over time, influenced and been influenced by developments in at least one of:	Covered in "developments" section of specification		
a) philosophical	Development: Pluralism and theology, Pluralism and Society Revealed Knowledge versus Natural Knoweldge	Natural theology and arguments for God's existence. Aquinas' Five Ways. 'Proofs' of God's existence. Logical Positivist verificationism.	Empiricism and its effects on ethics – rise of Utilitarianism. Links between Natural Theology and NL ethics.

b) ethical	Society: Gender and Society	Feminist critique of Religious Language.	Utilitarians as social reformers.
c) studies of religion			
d) textual interpretation	Society: Gender and Theology Liberation Theology as a new hermeneutic of oppression.	Religious Language. Bible as myth (Bultmann). Language as symbolic (Tillich)	Fletcher's hermeneutic – Jesus as a situationist, Parable of Good Samaritan.

The above detail is perhaps a little dense so let's put the Christian Thought specification into a list of linkages as we have done for the other two papers. We start with the Christian Thought section titles.

- Augustine – Plato. Augustine rejected Platonic theology from the Manichees, that there is separate good and evil and the body restricts the soul to a kingdom of darkness.

- Augustine – Plato. Plotinus instead believed in the Form of the Good alone, no good or evil aspects of the forms.

- Augustine – Problem of Evil. Evil is merely a privation (lack) of good.

- Augustine – Natural Law. Can't discover God through reason alone, need his Grace. Link with Calvin's sensus divinitatis in Natural and Revealed Theology, which is obscured by the Fall.

- Death and the Afterlife – Mind Body and Soul. Most Christians reject the idea that the body and soul separate after death and instead humans get a 'renewed spiritual body after death', as Paul argues in 1 Corinthians.

- Death and the Afterlife – Mind Body and Soul. St Paul believed in the tent analogy that our impermanent physical body would be replaced with a permanent 'spiritual body'.

- Death and the Afterlife – Augustine. Most Christians believe eternal life is given through the grace of God similar to Augustine's ideas of salvation from sin.

- Death and the Afterlife – Problem of Evil & Augustine. Bible and the Parable of the Sheep and the Goats supports the notion of evil merely being a privation of good. "What you didn't do to the least of these, you didn't do to me'.

- Death and the Afterlife – Body, Mind and Soul. Aristotle expands on his ideas surrounding different souls for different living things by arguing human souls are the only ones capable of surviving death – rational souls.

- Death and the Afterlife – Problem of Evil. Purgatory ideas supported by Hick in his 'vale of soul-making' after death.

- Natural+Revealed Theology of God - Natural Law etc. Poses the question of how knowledge can be gained, someone like Karl Barth would say this is only possible through scripture and revelation, whereas Aquinas would argue for nature plus reason as well.

- Natural+Revealed Theology of God – Natural Law. Both Aquinas and Polkinghorne emphasise the importance of unifying reason and faith.

- Natural+Revealed Theology of God – Cosmological/teleological arguments/natural Law. Both show that we can understand God by observing nature).

- Natural+Revealed Theology of God – Euthanasia. Everyone has a spark of divinity within them which not only allows them to be sacred but also be born with a sense of the Divine.

- Natural+Revealed Theology of God – Problem of Evil. Both introduce the ideas of epistemic distance. God is 'other' and 'beyond'.

- Natural+Revealed Theology of God – Religious Experience. Show that knowledge can be gained about God through immediate or mediate revelations.

- Person of Jesus – Body Mind and Soul. Rahner's onion analogy is very similar to Freud's psychodynamic theory; both suggest that there is a subconscious human layer that no one can reach.

- Person of Jesus – Religious Experience. Jesus's miracles also class as Religious experiences such as walking on water etc. Some are corporate, eg Feeding the 5,000, and some individual eg Healing the paralysed Man in Mark 2.

- Person of Jesus – Libertarian Theology. N.T Wright and Libertarian theologians both emphasise the importance of Jesus's tendency to involve the excluded members of society.

- Person of Jesus – Situation Ethics. Fletcher was inspired by Jesus's teachings of selfless agape).

- Person of Jesus – Death and the Afterlife. The quote from Matthew about the eye of the needle can be used alongside the Lazarus story." It is easier for a camel to fit through the eye of a needle then for a rich man to enter the kingdom of Heaven".

- Christian Moral Principles – Religious Experience/Natural Law. Some would argue that certain Religious Experiences are merely a sense of Jesus' presence and therefore non-propositional revelation. Non-propositional revelation also counts as gaining knowledge through reason, and so links to Natural Law in Ethics.

- Christian Moral Principles – Person of Jesus. Many bible-believing Christians face a problem as numerous texts from the Old Testament conflict with teachings from Jesus.

- Christian Moral Principles – Gender and Theology. Ruether and Daly point out issues with believing scripture as the books in the Bible are all described from a male perspective. Books from a female perspective such as Gospel of Mary Magdalene were suppressed.

- Christian Moral Principles – Person of Jesus/Situation Ethics. Bible-believing Christians have a high regard for Jesus' teachings on agape love.

- Christian Moral Principles – Link with Tillich on language as symbol in Religious Language (Philosophy of Religion).

- Christian Moral Action – Situation Ethics suggests that laws of the land can be broken if it fulfils a better human telos (purpose) of love.

- Christian Moral Action – Person of Jesus. Suffering was an essential element of Jesus's example, making it essential in Bonhoeffer's eyes in order to be a true Christian.

- Liberation Theology – Business Ethics. Liberation theology is a response to exploitation and alienation caused by globalisation.

- Liberation Theology – Person of Jesus. Jesus' focus on poor and outcasts.

- Liberation Theology and Situation ethics. Jospeh Fletcher started life as a Marxist and this influences his ethics eg "love and justice are the same' and 'justice is love distributed' (two of the six fundamental principles).

- Secularism – Marxism. Marx calls religion the 'opiate of the masses' to support the separation of Church and State.

- Secularism – Problem of Evil. Freud's quote about infantilism could be used for the Problem of Evil topic to support the notion that the problem only exists for a Christian worldview.

- Secularism – Euthanasia. Christianity influences governments in limiting people's freedoms.

- Secularism – Religious Experience. William James concluded that the purpose of religion is for people to live a more fulfilling and positive life.

- Gender and Theology – Person of Jesus. Ruether shows how Jesus challenged the warrior expectations and instead represented the idea of a Servant King.

- Gender and Theology – Augustine. Daly criticises Augustine along with others like Aquinas even though he said men and women were equal but men generally and naturally had superior roles.

- Gender and Theology – Christian Moral Action. Daly accuses Paul and Augustine of suggesting women must be subject to their husbands.

- Gender and Theology – Situation Ethics. Fletcher accused of creating an ethical system focused on individual liberation, and not the collective liberation of specific groups such as women.

- Gender and Theology – Sexual Ethics. Can use the concubine example from book of Judges to support/criticise the Church's position on abuse in sexual ethics.

- Gender and Theology – Person of Jesus. Daly cherry picks all the Bible parts which work for her argument and misses out the parts where Jesus supports equality of women e.g the story of the woman touching Jesus's cloak and no longer bleeding.

- Gender and Society – Aristotle. Aristotle's saw women being 'more easily moved to tears' etc. Aquinas said women are 'less rational'.

- Gender and Society – Plato/Body Mind and Soul. Plato specifies that only women are given souls by the Gods in his book Timaeus.

- Gender and Society – Gender and Theology. Catholic Mariology - doctrines of the Virgin Mary - says that fulfilment for a female involves either virginity or motherhood, whereas Daly would say females have better abilities and purposes. Link with feminist critique of Catholicism.

- Pluralism and Society – Gender and Society. Daly makes a correlation between war and the Bible. She then uses this to show how the Bible supports rape culture. However David Ford would suggest Christianity instead supports working together within a pluralist society.

- Pluralism and Theology – Augustine/Death and the Afterlife. The ideas of limited election, shared by Calvin and Augustine, would now be classed as narrow exclusivism.

- Pluralism and Theology – Religious Experience. Kraemer's belief that all other religions are cultural constructs seems similar to Feuerbacher's explanation that religion exists to create a more civilised society and allow humans to reach their full potential.

- Pluralism and Theology - Kant. Hick's universal pluralism is inspired by Kant's idea of the noumenal realm in ethics, which is inaccessible to direct human experience. This also links to Plato's forms of the good. Hick's pluralism ends up with no direct reference to Jesus (which he thinks makes it too exclusivist) but just to the one 'divine reality'. The 'divine reality' idea links to feminist Mary Daly's concept of Quintessence (a Medieval idea that there is an essence behind everything, which is quite postmodern and illustrations of this idea can be found in New Age spirituality).

How Assessment Works

Assessment is a mystery to most students and indeed, many teachers. This is because we believe (wrongly) that a grade awarded is an objective thing that doesn't change from year to year. We are understandably interested in our grade prediction because this is the basis of our University UCAS offer, But in fact we are assessed according to levels, not according to some objective standard of grade.

The process is as follows:

1. Your examiner receives your script on a screen and has already attended a session where the mark scheme is discussed. In practice this means that the examiners have outlines of indicative content. Indicative content just means the kind of content for which you would be awarded marks, rather than content that is wrong or irrelevant which will be ignored. But it is not prescriptive, in other words, it does not exclude many other ways of being awarded marks. So there is always an element of judgement and expertise required by examiners. Your examiner is repeatedly told to award marks positively and reward original, philosophical thinking.

2. The examiner has the levels in front of them and marks according to the levels. More about the levels in a moment, but here just be aware that levels are what we need to focus on, not grades. I realise that grades are what really interest you - so more about grades in a moment.

3. This gives you a raw mark for what are called AO1 criteria (knowledge and understanding) and AO2 criteria, (analysis and evaluation). At GCE A level the split is 40% AO1 and 60% AO2. So as the essay is marked out of 40, the AO1 marks are maximum 16

and the AO 2 marks are awarded up to a maximum of 24, making 40 in total.

4. The raw mark is then moderated and adjusted for grade boundaries. So if, say, the raw mark yields a total of 30/40 for a particular question and this is thought actually to be worth more marks, the marks will be adjusted upwards to, say, 35/40.

5. The grade boundaries are then applied to the adjusted marks. Generally (but not necessarily) the grade boundaries will be as follows:

A* 91% - 100%   36 marks and above

A 81% - 90%   32 marks - 36 marks

B 71% - 80%   28 marks - 32 marks

C 61% - 70%   24 marks - 28 marks

D 51% - 60%   20 marks - 24 marks

E 41% - 50%   16 marks - 20 marks

We will only know for sure after two or three years seeing how the marks and grades relate and whether (as is rumoured) fewer students proportionately will receive A* on this new specification.

From the preceding analysis we can see two things. Firstly, the mark range for each grade is very narrow - around 4 marks per grade per essay, marked out of 40. For this reason it is even more important to understand the levels discussed in the next section. Teachers must mark to the levels and students must understand how the levels translate into philosophical writing. My own experience suggest that this is where the problem lies: teachers may not understand how to teach to the levels, and students how to write to achieve the higher levels.

In other words, they don't necessarily understand what kind of writing will be rewarded, and how to teach to bring out these skills. The skills for higher level writing need to be broken down and built gradually step by step (I have just, with my colleagues, written three study guides, one for each paper, which show you how to do this. It's too big a question to answer how to do this in this book). We now turn to explain the levels themselves.

Explaining the Six Levels

The six levels at GCE A level (five at AS level) are designed to differentiate between students according to AO1 criteria (knowledge and understanding worth up to 40% or 16/40 marks) and AO2 criteria (analysis and evaluation worth 60% or 24/40 marks). In order to understand thee levels, we need a clear idea of what the key words 'excellent', 'very good', 'good', 'sound' actually mean and how they translate into an answer written in around 40 minutes under stressful exam conditions. Let's begin by focusing on Level 4 and then work upwards to level 6.

At AO1 level 4 we can gain between 8-10 marks for:

A good demonstration of knowledge and understanding in response to the question:

- *addresses the question well*

- *good selection of relevant material, used appropriately on the whole*

- *mostly accurate knowledge which demonstrates good understanding of the material used, which*

- *should have reasonable amounts of depth or breadth*

- *mostly accurate and appropriate use of technical terms and subject vocabulary.a good range of scholarly views, academic approaches, and/or sources of wisdom and authority are used to demonstrate knowledge and understanding*

Notice you will be awarded marks for your ability to address the question, and it needs to be done 'well'. Failure to discuss the question properly, a major misunderstanding of the question, deviation from the question in front of you: these are all reasons for dropping off level 4.

Secondly, you are awarded marks for your selection of material. This needs to be 'good' and this means you have identified the ideas and or scholars or the views to be set up in your answer and discussed. Taking up time discussing irrelevant people or irrelevant issues to the ones underlying the question are reasons for dropping off level 4.

Thirdly, the knowledge and understanding needs to be 'mostly accurate'. You can make some mistakes and misunderstand some of the ideas, you can be confused here and there. But major confusions, muddle and vagueness will see you fall off level 4.

Finally the technical terms used must be 'mostly accurate'. You can be inaccurate in places for level 4, but if you don't use technical vocabulary (such as the terms in the specification listed and explained in an appendix to this book) you will see yourself drop off level 4.

To repeat a point made earlier in the book, it is not a question of how many scholars you mention but how you handle scholarly views. The specification is crystal clear on this. Don't let your teacher force you into bad habits of listing scholars, rather than developing well-illustrated arguments.

At AO2 level 4 we can gain between 13 and 16 marks for:

A good demonstration of analysis and evaluation in response to the question:

- *argument is <u>generally successful</u> and <u>clear</u>*

- *<u>generally successful</u> analysis and evaluation*

- *views well stated, with <u>some development</u> and justification*

- *answers the question set <u>well</u>*

- *<u>mostly accurate</u> and <u>appropriate</u> use of technical terms and subject vocabulary.*

- *a <u>good range</u> of scholarly views, academic approaches and sources of wisdom and authority are used to support analysis and evaluation*

Assessment of Extended Response: There is a <u>well–developed line of reasoning</u> which is clear, relevant and logically structured.

Again, I have underlined some of the key words and phrases. If you are just making assertions or producing lists of points you will not be fulfilling the assessment of extended response criteria for a 'well-developed line of reasoning' and you will be falling off level 4. If there are several ambiguities and poor linkages in your argument, you will fall off level 4. If views are poorly developed, and present themselves as dogmatic, unqualified generalisations, you will fall off level 4. Moreover, if you deviate off the question in front of you or pass off a learnt answer as if the examiner won't notice it's learnt off by heart (a foolish strategy), you will also fall off level 4. Notice there is repetition between AO1 and AO2 on the last two bullet points.

What grade do we end up with if we write at the top end of level 4? We will be awarded 10 AO1 marks and 16 AO2 marks, giving us 26 marks out of 40. If this raw mark (see above) is not adjusted up or down for this question, then we will gain 65%, which is normally (but not necessarily, again, see my comments above) a grade C. You can be pretty good and yet only gain grade C - that is the stark position of today's candidate in full A level Religious Studies. So assuming you are reading this book because you want to attain A or A*, then what do we do to get up to level 5 or 6?

How to Gain Level 6

Having established that this new specification GCE A level is supposed to be harder, and having got a feel for level 4 marks, what does level 6 writing feel like?

Here are the criteria: notice how the word 'excellent' replaces the word 'good' and the ambiguities in writing, the confusions, the gaps, the irrelevance, the assertions, and the lack of a crystal clear sustained logic have all disappeared. You are thinking and writing like a philosopher and your timidity and over-reliance on the textbook has gone. Moreover, if your teacher is giving foolish advice such as 'you need to mention at least four scholars', then you are ignoring it because you realise it is sustained, scholarly, nuanced, logical, highly relevant answer that you are aiming for and achieving. Here are level 6 criteria:

AO1 Level 6 Knowledge and Understanding

- *fully comprehends* the demands of, and *focuses on,* the question throughout:

- *excellent selection* of relevant material which is skilfully used

- *accurate and highly detailed* knowledge which demonstrates *deep understanding* through a *complex and nuanced* approach to the material used

- *thorough, accurate* and precise use of technical terms and vocabulary in context

- *extensive range* of scholarly views, academic approaches, and/or sources of wisdom and authority are used to demonstrate knowledge and understanding

Notice how this highest level is demanding we show certain skills. We have realised that it is this question in front of us which we must attack and unpack with skill. If we aren't sure what the question means, we boldly dissect it in our terms, imposing clarity and logic on it. We know how to dig down into the sub-agendas which lurk in every philosophical question. We hark back to the integrating principles I mentioned in an earlier chapter. The selection of material is 'excellent', meaning, I don't throw all my knowledge down, but select those parts and make links to parts which build my case.

My deep understanding builds a 'complex and nuanced' case. As an empirical test, this means I use link words and phrases that show that I am not over-generalising (words like moreover, or however, or the phrase 'this assumes') demonstrate 'nuance'. 'Nuance' means I can detect subtlety and hidden meanings and assumptions, and I can make careful links and qualifications. I don't just blaze away making carefully-learnt generalisations. My knowledge is engaging and interesting in its selection, not monochrome and monotone. Above all it is guaranteed to wake the examiner up, not send them to sleep. There is an interesting quote, or an allusion to something that links synoptically which sharpens my knowledge up and makes it crystal clear. I have tried to post an example of an essay which fulfils these criteria in every section of the peped website for you to read if you want to feel how these broad categories flesh out in reality. What of AO2 criteria, the so-called 'higher order skills'?

AO2 Level 6 Analysis and Evaluation (21-24 marks)

- An *excellent demonstration* of analysis and evaluation in response to the question:

- *excellent, clear and successful argument*

- *confident and insightful critical analysis and detailed evaluation of the issue*

- *views skilfully and clearly stated, coherently developed and justified*

- *answers the question set precisely throughout*

- *thorough, accurate and precise use of technical terms and vocabulary in context*

- *extensive range of scholarly views, academic approaches and sources of wisdom and authority used to support analysis and evaluation*

Assessment of Extended Response: There is an excellent line of reasoning, well-developed and sustained, which is coherent, relevant and logically structured.

You can see that this type of essay will leap out at you for its successful, crystal clear, logical and compelling line of reasoning. The use of scholarly views is 'extensive', meaning there is more than one scholar or scholarly view cited. It's impossible to enumerate 'how many', however, because this entirely depends on the question and the selection required to establish a philosophical case. Analysis will be built into the sentence structure, the paragraphing and the links between paragraphs. The style will include use of analytical words and phrases, with qualifying words such as 'but' or 'however'. Analysis and evaluation will be sharpened up by the exposure of fallacies (mistakes in logic) and over-generalisations (like the slippery slope argument which is invariably an overstatement of some catastrophic outcome).

In short, this answer will be characterised by boldness and precision, and after reading the conclusion the examiner will exclaim, 'yes!' Point proven!Thesis established! Here is an answer that displays philosophical skill and insight.

Maybe (dare one hope for this?) this answer will actually say something new and original, make an association or an allusion which no other student has made. It will invoke film, literature or art, and show evidence that this student has become a culture-reader, able to interpret the signs of the times, and not pursue a textbook minimalism (inevitable because of the requirement to say a lot in a relatively few words, so losing nuance), like the C grade lemming.

How to Analyse Exam Questions

Past exam questions give us critical clues as to how the examiner interprets the specification. As indicated in the previous chapter, the specification is open-ended in many areas, and open to interpretation. What is certain is that no technical terms or authors will be mentioned in an exam question which aren't already mentioned in the syllabus.

The best approach to maximising A grade potential is to study carefully the trends in the questions, to examine which have been set before, and then relate them to the syllabus. Any areas that have never been examined before, or not for some time, are more likely to occur in the next paper set, as examiners have to range their questions across the whole syllabus and not stick to areas that may be easier to set questions on. So far we have the example questions published by the board and one set of GCE A level papers and two sets of AS level papers to consider. In so doing we need to pay attention to three points:

1. What is the wording of the question? Do any questions have unexpected twists to them, or are they really just re-wordings of the 'issues surrounding' sections of the specification? If the latter, then the exam has really become quite straightforward as we merely need to rewrite the 'issues surrounding' sections with appropriate trigger words announcing the direction of the question (discuss, evaluate etc).

2. No question can be set twice, including the specimen questions, so we can eliminate that question from any future list of predicted questions. However, the questions that are discussed in your textbook might be set, and indeed one was set in 2018 (Kantian ethics and business is in the Wilcockson and Wilkerson textbook, with suggestions on how to answer it).

3. There is a process of setting questions which involves using authorised trigger or command words, then wording a question so it is fair to the specification, and then suggesting indicative content and how to frame a mark scheme. We break this process down in the analysis that follows.

Command Words in Questions

The wording of all GCE A Level questions have a strong evaluative element within them. In fact the range of what are called 'command words' or 'trigger words' used in exam questions is narrow. These trigger words include:

Discuss

Evaluate

Contrast

Compare

Critically compare

Assess

Critically assess

To what extent

"Critically assess" or "critically compare" require you to weigh up arguments for this viewpoint and criticisms of the viewpoint (or two contrasting thinkers or viewpoints), and crucially, then say which you think are valid or invalid and why (notice you are always supposed to come to some sort of firm conclusion to achieve an A grade. It is never sufficient to say "there are strong arguments on both sides and so it ends up being a question of belief". Philosophy is always about developing a critical courage to come down in favour of one view or another (or one writer or another), with reasons.

As "critically compare" has only come as a command phrase once, it might be worth thinking which views could be compared within the syllabus. An obvious example is Aquinas' and Freud's view of conscience, as both are named in the ethics specification. In Philosophy of Religion you might be asked to 'critically compare the views of Ayer and Wittgenstein concerning the meaningfulness of religious language', and in Christian Thought, under secularism. 'critically compare Freud's and Dawkins' views of the origins and effects of religious belief'.

REVISION TIP - The more specific you make your revision the more useful it will be. For example, if you carefully revise Dawkins' and Freud's attack on the reasonableness of religious belief, and set it alongside that of Alister McGrath (who wrote 'the Dawkins Delusion' as a critique of such attacks), and learn some quotes for each view, then this detailed knowledge can be used for any question on secularism. Whereas if you only revise general arguments, you will be caught out when the examiner asks a question naming a specific philosopher listed in the specification.

A common trigger word is "Discuss". Of course, to discuss means to evaluate and to analyse, but a statement with discuss after it is more obviously biased one way or another. Illustrating this again from secularism in Christian Thought, the statement "God is a delusion, Discuss" is obviously biased against the evidence for the existence of God, and will involve a discussion of both the concept of "God" and the idea of what it means for some belief to be "a delusion".

REVISION TIP - Always practise unpacking key terms in an essay question, and do so critically. For example, the idea of God is ambiguous and open-ended, and Dawkins' description of God in his book The God Delusion might be described as a 'straw man' argument - meaning an artificial, biased, selective account which he sets up in order to ridicule and knock down.

"Evaluate" means to consider what is good or bad about a particular view, what is valid or invalid in an argument or what is strong or weak about an argument. As a philosophical point, 'invalidity' refers to deductive arguments (a priori arguments that move by logical steps from assumptions to conclusion, such as Anselm's ontological argument for the existence of God) whereas inductive arguments - those that come from observation, such as 'the sun will rise tomorrow' are actually arguments about evidence and probability. Evaluation can also take place at different stages of the argument, and close attention should be paid to these different stages. For example, we can evaluate **definitions** as ambiguous or clear, we can evaluate **assumptions** as valid or invalid, and we can evaluate **arguments** as strong or weak and **conclusions** as logically following or logically not following an argument. We can also take an evaluative stance on the statement in a discuss question itself, as they are often deliberately provocative, over-generalised, and loaded with assumptions.

REVISION TIP - Try to construct summary sheets that evaluate in this kind of way, by considering different definitions, the assumptions different philosophers make and the strength or otherwise of the argument that follows. Breaking it up this way forms a natural way of starting your essay. For example, in criticising Hume's analytic/synthetic divide in language, we could say "Hume's distinction is inadequate, his assumptions restrictive and the conclusion he therefore comes to is invalid". My revision guides all proceed in this way by **structures of thought,** which I believe makes them unique.

"To what extent" is may be used as a command phrase to begin the question. This invites the answer "to some extent" or "completely" or "not at all". For example, if we are asked to what extent God reveals himself through natural theology (Christian Thought, section on Knowledge of God), we will need to argue, either that nature is only one of several ways God reveals himself, or to say that it is the only way and as such a complete, final revelation of God, or that God doesn't reveal himself at all through nature - as Karl Barth believed and argued in his famous dispute with Karl Brunner which evoked the strong exclamation 'nein!' (no!).

"To what extent" also invites a consideration of what exactly it is about God we can see in the revelation of the Bible: God's character, actions, view of humanity and creation, the things God hates and loves: these are all relevant and require practice in taking a line on a question. The Oxford academic Alister McGrath argues strongly that the whole division between natural and revealed theology is misguided, and of course, that it depends what we mean by 'natural theology' which he defines in a very particular way. His argument is that natural theology took a wrong turning in the Enlightenment (sixteenth to eighteenth centuries) in attempting to prove God exists; rather natural theology is a 'fiduciary framework' just as valid as Dawkins' empiricist framework as both are attempts to provide a holistic way of seeing all reality, including the metaphysical.

Philosophy of Religion Exam Questions H573/1

THE QUESTIONS WE HAVE SO FAR

1. *To what extent is the ontological argument successful in proving the existence of God? [40] Specimen Question 2016*

2. *To what extent does Hume successfully argue that observation does not prove the existence of God? (OCR GCE 2018 Q.2)*

3. *'Religious experience shows that we can be united with something greater than ourselves.' Discuss. [40] OCR Specimen Question 2016*

4. *Evaluate the view that the thinking mind is separate from the body. [40] OCR Specimen Question 2016*

5. *Critically compare the via negativa with symbolic language as ways of expressing religious beliefs in words. (40) OCR Specimen Paper 2016*

6. *'The best approach to understanding religious language is through the Cataphatic Way.' Discuss. (OCR GCE 2018 Q.1)*

7. *'Corporate religious experiences are less reliable than individual religious experience.' Discuss. (OCR GCE 2018 Q.4)*

8. *Assess Boethius' view that divine eternity does not limit human free will. (OCR GCE 2018 Q.3)*

We know that a very large number of students attempted Q.1 in the 2018 exam (Q.6 in my list above). A fair proportion muddled up the anaphatic and cataphatic ways in their answer. Let's be clear: its an entirely fair and predictable question, and also let's be clear, as the terms are clearly listed in the specification there is no excuse for not knowing them or muddling them up. Teachers who protested about this question have no basis for their protest at all.

That said, the examiner will simply flip your answer if you did this with otherwise perfectly clear analysis and good evaluation. The examiner will simply read it as if you had put the word 'cataphatic' where you have 'anaphatic' with the correct interpretation of the terms. The anxiety this question produced was largely misplaced. However, as it was the first paper it might well have seriously undermined the confidence of some students and if we are teachers, it is our job to point out the groundlessness of the anxiety so produced.

It was felt to be the hardest of the three papers set in 2018, partly because of the wording of question 2, which asks:

To what extent does Hume successfully argue that observation does not prove the existence of God? (OCR GCE 2018 Q.2)

Notice two things that make this hard. First it has the phrase 'to what extent' which I think is the hardest of the command words/phrases. It requires a big element of nuance to answer this effectively, as the alternatives are - to some extent (what is necessary to be explained of course), to no extent (with very solid grounds for rejecting all of Hume's argument), or to a complete extent (meaning you totally agree with Hume, but you need to consider some counter-arguments to Hume's view along the way, and reject them). All this means you need a very good command of Hume's argument and counter-arguments to it, and to have formed your own view, fully justifying it along the way.

A second reason it is relatively challenging is the negative in the question, 'does not prove the existence of God'. Negatives are always harder to get your brain around.

Now I mentioned a while back that we can turn to the full and very helpful list of issues around each topic area. In this section of the specification on the Existence of God, Arguments Based on Observation, the specification outlines content on challenges to the arguments from observation (or teleological/design and cosmological/first cause arguments, as we normally refer to them) and then cites Hume in these words:

Details of Hume's criticisms of these arguments for the existence of God from natural religion (OCR Specification, 2016, Philosophy of Religion H573/1)

Notice the reference to natural religion which echoes the Knowledge of God section in the Christian Thought specification, on revealed and natural theology, and the ethical theory of natural law. On the issues surrounding this part of the Philosophy of Religion specification, it states:

Learners should have the opportunity to discuss issues related to arguments for the existence of God based on observation, including:

- *whether a posteriori or a priori is the more persuasive style of argument*

- *whether or not teleological arguments can be defended against the challenge of 'chance'*

- *whether cosmological arguments simply jump to the conclusion of a transcendent creator, without sufficient explanation*

- *whether or not there are logical fallacies in these arguments that cannot be overcome (OCR Philosophy of Religion H573/1)*

Hume attacks the arguments from natural religion for three reasons:

1. The evidence is ambiguous and only suggest at best a rather puny God who left the business of a perfect creation unfinished.

2. Hume's strategy is to leave the reader with the (false) impression that the teleological argument must alone supply the premises for all natural theological conclusions about God; he then (easily) demonstrates that it collapses under this burden; thus (he thinks) he discredits traditional natural theology.

3. He thinks the cosmological argument is riddled with fallacies and so the teleological argument is the only one worth considering.

As an exercise on writing exam questions with trigger words and phrases, I produced a list before the exam was held. Here is what I came up with for this section:

- *'The teleological argument proves that the universe is designed.' Discuss.*

- *Assess Hume's challenges to the teleological argument.*

- *Critically evaluate a priori against a posteriori arguments for God's existence.*

- *Can teleological arguments be successfully defended against the challenge of 'chance' and natural selection?*

You can see, I think, that if you put the precise wording of the specification, the issues that are then listed from this part of the specification, and the key trigger words or phrases, it is fairly easy to predict a question which is almost the same as the one set in 2018. All we have to do is to do this exercise for the whole of the Philosophy of Religion specification. What follows is my complete list for this paper H573/1 - use it as a checklist from year to year and also to check that you can do all the questions listed here. Forewarned is, as often happens in life, as in exams, really to be forearmed.

The Complete List of Possible Exam Questions - Philosophy of Religion

Here (with the help of my colleagues) I have taken the specification and turned it into possible future exam questions. Our advice is to play careful attention to this list: it is highly likely you will get questions very similar to four of these in your actual exam.

Plato – the Cave/Forms

1. Critically compare Plato's Form of the Good with Aristotle's Prime Mover.

2. "In their attempts to make sense of reality, Plato relies too much on rationalism and Aristotle relies too much on empirical observation". Discuss

3. Assess the claim that Plato does not value experience enough.

4. 'Plato's Theory of Forms explains how we know what we know.' Discuss

Aristotle – Empiricism

5. 'Aristotle successfully proves the existence of the Prime Mover.' Discuss.

6. Assess Aristotle's argument for the Four Causes.

7. "Aristotle's reliance on empiricism has many weaknesses". Discuss

8. Evaluate whether Plato's rationalism is superior to Aristotle's empiricism in making sense of reality.

Soul – Mind, Body, Spirit

9. Assess the claim that disembodied existence is possible.

10. "The body is separate from the soul." Discuss

11. "The concept of the soul is best understood as a metaphor." Discuss

12. "The mind/body distinction is a category error." Evaluate this view.

Soul, Body, Mind, Spirit – Monism

13. "The body and soul cannot be separated." Discuss.

14. Assess whether the soul is best considered as reality or as metaphor.

15. Evaluate what Aristotle meant by arguing that the soul is the form of the body.

16. "The body dies, but the soul lives forever". Discuss

Ontological Argument

17. 'Anselm's Ontological Argument proves God exists logically.' Discuss.

18. Assess the claim that existence is a predicate.

19. "A priori arguments for God's existence are more persuasive than a posteriori arguments". Discuss

20. Critically evaluate the view that the ontological argument contains a number of logical fallacies which nullify the conclusion that God exists.

Cosmological Argument

21. Assess the claim that the cosmological argument proves that God exists a posteriori.

22. Hume's challenges successfully disprove the cosmological argument.' Discuss.

23. "The cosmological argument jumps to the conclusion that there is a transcendental creator without sufficient explanation". Discuss

24. "Aquinas' first three ways provide compelling reasons to believe in God". Discuss

Teleological Argument

25. 'The teleological argument proves that the universe is designed.' Discuss.

26. Assess Hume's challenges of the teleological argument.

27. Critically evaluate a priori against a posteriori arguments for God's existence.

28. Can teleological arguments be successfully defended against the challenge of 'chance' and natural selection?

Religious Experience

29. Assess the claim that religious experiences prove that God exists.

30. 'Religious experiences are nothing more than forms of psychological neurosis.' Discuss.

31. "Personal testimony can never be reliable evidence for God's existence". Discuss

32. Critically compare corporate religious experiences with individual experiences as a basis for belief in God.

Problem of Evil

33. 'There is no solution to the problem of evil and suffering.' Discuss.

34. Assess the success of John Hick's argument for soul-making as a development of Irenaeus' theodicy.

35. Assess which logical or evidential aspects of the problem of evil pose the greatest challenge to belief.

36. Critically assess whether it is possible to defend monotheism in the face of the existence of evil.

Nature of God

37. Critically assess the philosophical problems raised by believing in an omnibenevolent God.

38. Evaluate the philosophical problems raised by the belief that God is eternal.

39. Assess the claim that the universe shows no evidence of the existence of a benevolent God.

40. Critically assess the problems for believers who say that God is omniscient.

41. Boethius was successful in his argument that God rewards and punishes justly. Discuss.

42. Critically assess the philosophical problems raised by belief that God is omniscient.

Classical Religious Language

43. To what extent is the Via Negativa the only way to talk about God?

44. Evaluate the claim that analogy can successfully be used to express the human understanding of God.

45. Critically assess the views of Paul Tillich on religious language.

Religious Language – Twentieth Century Approaches

46. Critically assess Wittgenstein's belief that language games allow religious statements to have meaning.

47. The falsification principle presents no real challenge to religious belief. Discuss

48. Critically assess the claim that religious language is meaningless.

Mark Schemes and Indicative Content - Philosophy of Religion H573/1

Indicative content is merely suggestions of some possible approaches to scoring AO1 and AO2 marks. It is not meant to be an exhaustive approach. The nearer a candidate is to scoring A* the more likely it is they will be bold enough to depart from these suggestions and form original, interesting and highly relevant examples of knowledge and evaluation. Part of the skill to learn is moral courage: the courage to think incisively and critically as a philosopher. This skill can be taught and practised.

Below I make detailed comments on one of the questions and the examiner's guide to indicative content. Guidance for the the other questions in the Specimen Paper 2016 and the 2018 paper are downloadable from the OCR website. My comments are in italics.

2 'Religious experience shows that we can be united with something greater than ourselves.' Discuss. [40] OCR Specimen Question 2016

AO1 Candidates may demonstrate knowledge and understanding through the use of some of the following materials:

reference might be made to one or a number of kinds of religious experience, such as mystical, corporate and conversion

These need careful handling as we need to be clear about the differences between them and whether corporate religious experiences are a separate category from individual or just another form of an individual experience. An individual experience would be something like the mystical visions of St Teresa of Avila. A corporate experience would be something like the Toronto blessing (or in the Bible what happened on the first day of Pentecost described in Acts). Be aware, too, that there isn't necessarily one definition of 'corporate religious experience', as with many terms of technical vocabulary, and you need to unpick the terms carefully.

description and explanation of religious experience using William James' approach:

• the principles of pluralism, empiricism and pragmatism

Again, handle and research these terms with care. They don't mean the same thing as pragmatism in situation ethics or empiricism to AJ Ayer.

- his conclusions that the primacy of religious experience should be distanced from the secondary belief or structures of organised religion

I'm not sure how this point relates to the question and any point made needs to be explicitly related back to the question.

- some candidates may recognise an echo of James' conclusions in the phrasing of the question

Interesting point, needs to be spelt out.

negative approaches to religious experience might be explained

alternative approaches to religious experience, for example those provided by physiology, sociology, psychology or others, might be selected and applied relevantly

You could link this to views of Freud which form part of Christian Thought, Secularism, expressed in the Future of an Illusion which sees religion as infantile neurosis caused by projection on to a father figure, God. Neuroses can easily transform into ecstatic experiences, especially if the person has a big anxiety complex which is suddenly 'taken away' by a step of self-belief or self-delusion.

AO2 Candidates may demonstrate evaluation and analysis through the use of some of the following arguments: they might argue that religious experience does provide the basis for belief that we can be united with something greater than ourselves, because:

- if the individual subject of the experience is reliable, and their account considered trustworthy, then this might be considered to be strong evidence of the divine and/or union with a greater power

- individuals' descriptions of their personal religious experiences could be argued to be a legitimate description of a personal experience of the divine/unification with a greater power

- if a range of experiences are identified, then the weight of evidence presented could support the conclusion expressed in the question candidates might choose to argue, to the contrary, that religious experiences do not show the possibility of our unity with something greater than ourselves, because:

- if religious experience of the divine is beyond humanity, or we accept a non-interventionist approach to divine activity in the world, then apparent religious experiences do not suggest the possibility of unification with something greater, as these accounts would not be considered reliable or legitimate

- a sceptical or atheistic approach might be adopted, which questions the validity of religious experiences, possibly using disciplines such as physiology, sociology, psychology or others.

My general point would be this: the quote is value-laden which we are being asked to discuss. It implies that religious experiences are different from, and stand separate from ordinary human experiences, which I think is doubtful. Is falling in love with Christ so very different from the mystical experience of falling in love generally? Secondly it implies that religious experiences can show or prove something. But by what criteria do we verify religious experiences as authentic forms of divine experience? Surely this kind of discussion should form part of the indicative content which seems rather general and AO1-ish to me. A* candidates always go hard at the sub-agenda, the hidden assumptions behind questions - and by so doing produce a much more highly evaluated, critical analysis.

Ethics Exam Questions H573/2

Questions so Far - Ethics

1. *'Ethical terms are meaningless.' Discuss. (OCR Specimen Paper 2016)*

2. *Conscience is just the super-ego.' Discuss. (OCR Specimen Paper 2016)*

3. *Assess the view that utilitarianism provides the best approach to business ethics. (OCR Specimen Paper 2016)*

4. *Assess the view that situation ethics is of no help with regard to the issue of euthanasia. (OCR Specimen Paper 2016)*

5. *Assess the view that Natural Law is of no help with regard to the issue of euthanasia. (OCR Paper H573/2 2018 Q1)*

6. *'Kantian ethics provide the best approach to business ethics.' Discuss. (OCR Paper H573/2 2018 Q2)*

7. *'"Good" is meaningful.' Discuss. (OCR Paper H573/2 2018 Q3)*

8. *Evaluate Aquinas' theological approach to conscience. (OCR Paper H573/2 2018 Q4)*

The 2018 Ethics paper H573/2, which is the only paper we have as I write this, seems to have no obvious twists or problems. The only problem word is the word 'theological' in question 4 of the paper (question 8 above). A candidate who simply ignores this word and talks about Aquinas' theory of conscience will be falling off an A grade straightaway. We must practise unpacking and giving content to all aspects of the exam question in front of us. 'Theological' here simply means 'coming from God and orientated towards the good by synderesis, a gift of God". Synoptically we can link this to design arguments and the idea of the eternal law in natural law theory, and natural theology in Knowledge of God (Christian Thought) . The eternal law is one of the four laws Aquinas mentioned. In some ways the eternal law is like Plato's FORMS of the good - they exist as a perfect blueprint for creation in the mind of God which is only accessible by natural religion or natural law in ethics, and by revelation or the divine law in the Bible. Human reason or ratio is our God-given ability either by intuition (intellectus) or by working things out (ratio, as applied in scientific research for example) in order to get some grasp of God's eternal law. Does the specification mention the theological theory of Aquinas?

Indeed it does: the specification lists clearly Aquinas' theological approach as required knowledge, and then enumerates five areas to consider:

Details of this theological approach, including:

- *ratio (reason placed in every person as a result of being created in the image of God)*

- *synderesis (inner principle directing a person towards good and away from evil)*

- *conscientia (a person's reason making moral judgements).*

- *vincible ignorance (lack of knowledge for which a person is responsible)*

- *invincible ignorance (lack of knowledge for which a person is not responsible)*

Then under the issues to consider section of this part of the specification we find further helpful elaboration:

Learners should have the opportunity to discuss issues related to ideas about conscience, including:

- *comparison between Aquinas and Freud:*

- *on the concept of guilt*

- *on the presence or absence of God within the workings of the conscience and super-ego*

- *on the process of moral decision-making*

- *whether conscience is linked to, or separate from, reason and the unconscious mind*

- *whether conscience exists at all or is instead an umbrella term covering various factors involved in moral decision-making, such as culture, environment, genetic predisposition and education*

How did my suggestions, posted on the peped site, square up against the questions that were actually asked on the day? Here is my list:

Critically evaluate the theories of conscience of Aquinas and Freud.

"Conscience is given by God, not formed by childhood experience". Critically evaluate this view with reference to Freud and Aquinas.

"Conscience is a product of culture, environment, genetic predisposition and education" . Discuss

"Conscience is another word for irrational feelings of guilt". Discuss

"Freud's theory of conscience has no scientific basis. It is merely hypothesis". Discuss

'Guilt feelings are induced by social relationships as a method of control".
Discuss

Is Conscience linked to or separate from reason and the unconscious mind?

You can see that whilst I didn't ask about Aquinas' theological theory of conscience using the word 'theological', the issues you need to unpack for a successful answer to the 2018 exam question are fully implicit in these suggestions So practise these questions and you will definitely be successful in gaining an A grade.

The Full List of Possible Questions

Here is a full list of possible questions for the Ethics exam based on both the content and suggestions for issues to explore, found in the specification H573/2. It is a good idea to try answering as many of these as you can, concentrating on the ones you find hardest.

Natural Law

1. "Natural Law does not present a helpful method for making moral decisions". Discuss

2. "Moral decisions should be based on duty, not purpose". Assess with reference to the theory of Natural Law.

3. "Human beings are born with the tendency to pursue morally good ends". Evaluate in the light of teleological aspects of Natural Law.

4. "Explain and justify the doctrine of double effect with reference to an ethical dilemma of your choice concerning euthanasia".

5. Critically assess the view that natural law is the best approach to issues surrounding sexual ethics.

Kant

6. "Kantian ethics is helpful in providing practical guidelines for making moral decisions in every context". Discuss

7. Evaluate to what extent duty can be the sole basis for a moral action.

8. "Kantian ethics is too abstract to be useful in practical ethical decision-making'. Discuss

9. "In neglecting the role of emotions in favour of pure reason, Kantian ethics fails to give a realistic account for our human nature". Discuss

Utilitarianism

10. Evaluate the view that utilitarianism does not provide a helpful way of solving moral dilemmas.

11. To what extent, if any, is Utilitarianism a useful theory for approaching moral decisions in life? (Patrick King)

12. Utilitarianism provides a helpful method of moral decision making. Discuss Already marked

13. The application of the greatest happiness principle in specific situations is not a sufficient guide to the good action". Discuss

14. "Pleasure is not quantifiable". Discuss

15. To what extent does utilitarian ethics provide a useful guide to issues surrounding business ethics?

Situation Ethics

16. "Situation ethics is too demanding as a system of ethical decision-making". Discuss

17. "Goodness is only defined by asking – how is agape best served". Discuss

18. "Agape is not so much a religious idea as an equivalent to saying 'I want the best for you'". Discuss

19. Evaluate the extent to which situation ethics is individualistic and subjective.

Applied – Euthanasia (Natural Law and Situation Ethics)

20. Natural Law is superior to situation ethics in its treatment of issues surrounding euthanasia". Discuss

21. Natural law succeeds because it takes human nature seriously. Discuss

22. "Autonomy as an ideal is unrealistic. No-one is perfectly autonomous". Discuss with reference to the ethical issue of euthanasia.

23. "Sanctity of human life is the core principle of medical ethics". Discuss

24. "There is no moral difference between actively ending a life by euthanasia and omitting to treat the patient". Discuss

Applied – Business Ethics (Kant and Utilitarianism)

25. "Kantian ethic of duty is superior to the utilitarian ethic of happiness in dealing with difficult business decisions". Discuss

26. Critically discuss the view that businesses have a moral duty to put their customers first.

27. "Corporate social responsibility is ethical window-dressing to cover their greed". Discuss

28. Evaluate the view that capitalism will always exploit human beings in the pursuit of profit.

29. "Globalisation widens the exploitation of human beings by reducing the need for ethically valid regulation of business behaviour". Discuss

Meta-ethics

31. "The meaning of the word 'good' is the defining question in the study of ethics". Discuss

32. Critically consider whether ethical terms such as good, bad, right and wrong have an objective factual basis that makes them true or false.

33. "Ethical statements are merely an expression of an emotion". Discuss

34. Evaluate the view that ethical statements are meaningless.

35. "People know what's right or wrong by a common sense intuition". Discuss

36. Critically contrast the views of intuitionists and emotivists on the origin and meaning of ethical statements.

Conscience

37. Critically evaluate the theories of conscience of Aquinas and Freud.

38. "Conscience is given by God, not formed by childhood experience". Critically evaluate this view with reference to Freud and Aquinas.

39. "Conscience is a product of culture, environment, genetic predisposition and education". Discuss

40. "Conscience is another word for irrational feelings of guilt". Discuss

41. "Freud's theory of conscience has no scientific basis. It is merely hypothesis". Discuss

42. 'Guilt feelings are induced by social relationships as a method of control". Discuss

43. Is Conscience linked to or separate from reason and the unconscious mind?

Sexual Behaviour

44. "In terms of sexual ethical decisions, all you need to do is apply your conscience". Discuss

45. "Religion is irrelevant in deciding issues surrounding sexual behaviour". Discuss

46. Critically evaluate the view that the ethics of sexual behaviour should be entirely private and personal.

47. "Because sexual conduct affects others, it should be subject to legislation". Discuss

48. "Normative theories are useful in what they might say about sexual ethics". Discuss

Mark Schemes and Indicative Content - Ethics

There has only been one mark scheme produced as I write this, the scheme for the specimen paper of 2016. The board states very clearly: 'the following is a description of possible content only; all legitimate answers and approaches must be credited appropriately. Learners are expected to make use of scholarly views, academic approaches and sources of wisdom and authority to support their argument'. The first full examiners' report should appear in the autumn of 2018 - and would be a good document to research and study.

Below I make detailed comments on one of the questions and the examiner's guide to indicative content. Guidance for the the other questions in the Specimen Paper 2016 and the 2018 paper are downloadable from the OCR website. My comments are in italics.

1. *Assess the view that utilitarianism provides the best approach to business ethics. (OCR Specimen Paper 2016)*

The following is a description of possible content only; all legitimate answers and approaches must be credited appropriately. Learners are expected to make use of scholarly views, academic approaches and sources of wisdom and authority to support their argument.

We have the catch-all get out comment that anything relevant will be assessed and credited accordingly. So again, be wary of suggested ways of answering questions which close off other ways equally valid and sometimes more interesting than the obvious one. We should always try to say something interesting, even unique or unusual.

AO1 Candidates may demonstrate knowledge and understanding through the use of some of the following:

in discussing business ethics candidates may explain or mention all or some of the following:

- corporate social responsibility (that a business has responsibility towards the community and environment)

Remember that there is an underlying issue in all ethics, what happens when two moral goods conflict? Here the obligations to shareholder and to local community are often in direct conflict, and you can't fulfil both. Shareholders want profit and dividends paid out on their investment and the local community wants a nice environment, clean air, and no waste products. Keeping a clean environment costs money as Trafigura found in the 2006 example when they tried to save money by dumping toxic waste in the Ivory Coast.

- whistle-blowing (that an employee discloses wrongdoing to the employer or the public)

- globalisation (that around the world economies, industries, markets, cultures and policy-making is integrated)

Again there may be conflicts in an ethical approach to globalisation concerning health and safety standards, workers rights and of course, workers pay. for an example of poor health and safety standards research the Rana Plaza disaster where a factory supplying a Canadian company with cheap textile goods collapsed in Bangladesh.

in discussing utilitarianism and its application candidates may explain or mention some or all of the following:

- utility (what will offer the greatest happiness to the greatest number of people)

- the hedonic calculus (a method of calculating the benefit or harm of an act through its consequences)

119

- act utilitarianism (calculating the consequences of each situation on its own merits)

- rule utilitarianism (following accepted laws that maximise the happiness of everyone)

candidates may also provide details of other normative theories, most likely that of Kant, in order to compare them to utilitarianism in their application.

This is an important point: it is wise when the question uses the word 'best' as in 'best approach' to contrast one theory with another. The deontological, absolute theory of Kant is in vivid contrast to the more experience-based, pleasure and pain calculation of the utilitarians. For a further case study on utilitarian calculation research the Ford Pinto case in the USA in 1973, on the peped website.

AO2 Candidates may demonstrate evaluation and/or analysis through the use of some of the following arguments: candidates might assess that utilitarianism provides the best approach to business ethics using some of the following reasons:

- utilitarianism is based on the extent to which, in any given situation, utility is best served; this might be argued to be a common sense approach suited to business

'Common sense' is a dangerous phrase in ethics which I would avoid. Of course, it depends crucially on my wisdom and ability to assess consequences whether utilitarianism works at all. It also has a very pragmatic approach, for example, that we can employ lax safety standards as long as no-one knows and no-one dies. There is an 'ignorance is bliss' element here as British consumers are quite happy to buy low priced Primark goods as long as no great scandal (such as child labour) attaches to their production.

- according to the hedonic calculus and Bentham's act utilitarianism, principles and laws have to be considered only insofar as they provide utility and beneficial consequences, meaning there is flexibility to allow good business decisions

I would say that Bentham's hedonic calculus is a weird seven-fold classification of how to measure pleasure which makes no sense in reality and is useless for business or anyone else. Bentham's theory is individualistic and hedonic (pleasure-based) and this examiner's comment would better fit Mill's weak rule utilitarianism.

- the view that in business ethics utilitarianism provides the best approach because according to rule utilitarianism, principles and laws have to be accepted, meaning businesses cannot act completely outside of accepted rules

There is an element of pragmatic flexibility in Mill's approach because he argues for two levels of judgement - generally follow rules that admit of the greatest happiness, based on past experience, but go back to being an act utilitarian where two goods conflict. There is a practical realism here. There is also less emphasis on the individual constantly having to calculate which mars Bentham's theory.

- the view that utilitarianism in general provides the best approach as it might accept corporate social responsibility because this maximises utility for the all stakeholders, not just for employers or shareholders intent on maximising profits

- the view that utilitarianism in general provides the best approach as it might accept globalisation as the spread of capitalism enable humans to flourish whilst consumerism provides the opportunity to maximise pleasure

candidates might assess that utilitarianism does not provide the best approach to business ethics based on some of the following possible reasons:

- since the overall goal of business is making profits, the best approach is simply the one that focuses on the maximisation of profits

Big assumption here, that the consumer is happy just in focusing on price, rather than the environmental impact etc. Ethical consumerism is actually on the rise as we see with the purchase of expensive electric cars.

- it is too flexible to ensure businesses are held to account and are not able to simply justify whatever they want

The idea of flexibility is not connected to 'being held to account' so this point is too fuzzy to be of any use to us.

- it is teleological and based on consequences, which are not necessarily predictable, meaning it is not a helpful approach

Mill's version is only partly consequentialist because it is the wisdom of past players who determine the general rules - so again don't write like this if you want an A*. Mill's point is that it's easier for all of us to navigate by the wisdom of past experience than be involved in making constant calculations required by act utilitarianism.

- the hedonic calculus is too long and complex a method to use in making real world decisions.

- candidates may compare utilitarianism in its application to another normative theory, most likely that of Kant, and conclude that the alternative provides a better approach, for example:

Kantian ethics provides a better/best approach because it is based on duty rather than utility

Kantian ethics through the formula of the law of nature provides a better/best approach because it encourages whistle-blowing as a duty regardless of utility or consequences.

Kantian ethics through the formula of the end in itself provides a better/best approach because it ensures the rights of employees and consumers.

Christian Thought Exam Questions H573/3

Past Questions so Far - Christian Thought

For GCE level we have one specimen paper and one actual paper to go on so far. Here are the list of questions - remember no question can ever be used again in this form.

1. *'Secularists who say Christianity is a source of unhappiness are wrong.' Discuss. (OCR Specimen Paper 2016)*

2. *'Christianity is not the only means to salvation.' Discuss. (OCR Specimen Paper 2016)*

3. *Assess whether Christianity and feminism are compatible. (OCR Specimen Paper 2016)*

4. *'Hell is an idea not a place'. Discuss (OCR Specimen Paper 2016)*

5. *To what extent was Jesus merely a political liberator? (OCR H573/3 2018 Q1)*

6. *'Bonhoeffer's theology is still relevant today.' Discuss. (OCR H573/3 2018 Q2)*

7. *Assess the view that Mary Daly's theology proves that Christianity is sexist. (OCR H573/3 2018 Q3)*

8. *Secularism does not pose a threat to Christianity.' Discuss. (OCR H573/3 2018 Q4)*

Let's analyse one of these questions to see how it coheres with the specification and to evaluate the extent to which it might have been predicted. The question on Bonhoeffer states:

'Bonhoeffer's theology is still relevant today.' Discuss. (OCR H573/3 2018 Q2)

This falls within the Moral Action part of the Christian Thought specification. The content asks us to consider:

- *The teaching and example of Dietrich Bonhoeffer on:*

- *duty to God and duty to the State*

- *Church as community and source of spiritual discipline*

- *the cost of discipleship*

Key knowledge in the specification includes the following requirements:

- *Bonhoeffer's teaching on the relationship of Church and State including:*

- *obedience, leadership and doing God's will*

- *justification of civil disobedience*

- *Bonhoeffer's role in the Confessing Church and his own religious community at Finkenwalde*

- *Bonhoeffer's teaching on ethics as action, including:*

- *'costly grace'*

- *sacrifice and suffering*

- *solidarity*

Notice so far there is no specific reference in the specification as to whether or not Bonhoeffer's theology is relevant for us today. Notice also that key word is 'relevant". Relevant to whom and for what purpose? Presumably of little relevance to the atheist (but even that all depends) or those living in untroubled times (depending what we consider 'troubled'). Notice also a golden thread of liberation from oppression in this paper, in this case the oppression of a barbarous Nazi regime, which unites both Bonhoeffer and the feminist theologians and liberation theologians. Like the liberationist, Bonhoeffer's is a theology of martyrdom. To follow Christ is to embrace the possibility of dying for righteousness and justice. So is there reference in the suggested issues for guidance. which is also part of the specification? Here's what they are:

Learners should have the opportunity to discuss issues related to Christian moral action in the life and teaching of Bonhoeffer, including:

- *whether or not Christians should practise civil disobedience*

- *whether or not it is possible always to know God's will*

- *whether or not Bonhoeffer puts too much emphasis on suffering*

- *whether or not Bonhoeffer's theology has relevance today*

So again we have a clear signal in this fourth bullet point indicating areas and issues to study which clearly states that 'relevance today' is something we need to consider. Failure to notice these links is of course a further serious error. (Remember earlier I suggested that anyone not throughly learning technical vocabulary is simply shooting their A grade prospects in the foot).

What then were the suggested possible questions on this section in my 2018 list produced before the exam, and did they anticipate this question?

"Using the will of God as a guide for moral behaviour is impractical, as in most circumstances it is impossible to know what God wants us to do." Discuss.

To what extent, if at all, does the theology of Bonhoeffer have relevance for Christians today?

"Bonhoeffer's most important teaching is on leadership." Discuss.

"Christian ethics means being obedient to God's will." Discuss.

To what extent was Bonhoeffer's religious community at Finkenwalde successful?

Again, we can see that by following a simple strategy of playing close attention to the clues in the specification, and then adding possible trigger or command words or phrases, we can anticipate likely questions and arm ourselves thoroughly. Here the word 'relevant' needs to be fully and critically unpacked rather than its meaning just assumed. It is by no means clear what it means, and part of our developing examination skill is to impose our own individual line upon it.

Full List of Possible Exam Questions - Christian Thought

Augustine

1. Assess the view that Augustine's teaching on human nature is too pessimistic

2. Critically assess the view that Christian teaching on human nature can only make sense if the Fall did actually happen

3. "Augustine's teaching on human nature is more harmful than helpful". Discuss.

4. How convincing is Augustine's teaching about the Fall and Original Sin?

5. Critically assess Augustine's analysis of human sexual nature

Death and the Afterlife

6. To what extent can belief in the existence of purgatory be justified?

7. "Heaven is not a place but a state of mind." Discuss.

8. "Without the reward of Heaven Christians would not behave well." Discuss

9. To what extent is the Parable of the Sheep and the Goats in Matthew 25 only about Heaven and Hell?

10. Assess the view that there is no last judgement; each person is judged by God at the moment of their death.

11. "Purgatory is the most important Christian teaching about the afterlife." Discuss.

Knowledge of God

12. Discuss critically the view that Christians can discover truths about God using human reason.

13. "Faith is all that is necessary to gain knowledge of God." Discuss.

14. "God can be known because the world is so well designed." Discuss.

15. Critically assess the view that the Bible is the only way of knowing God.

16. "Everyone has an innate knowledge of God's existence." Discuss.

17. To what extent is faith in God rational?

Person of Christ

18. "There is no evidence to suggest that Jesus thought of himself as divine." Discuss.

19. To what extent can Jesus be regarded as no more than a teacher of wisdom?

20. "Jesus' role was just to liberate the poor and weak against oppression." Discuss.

21. Assess the view that the miracles prove Jesus was the Son of God.

22. "Jesus Christ is not unique." Discuss.

23. To what extent was Jesus just a teacher of morality?

Christian Moral Principles

24. How fair is the claim that there is nothing distinctive about Christian ethics?

25. "The Bible is all that is needed as a moral guide for Christian behaviour." Discuss.

26. "The Church should decide what is morally good." Discuss.

27. Assess the view that the Bible is a comprehensive moral guide for Christians.

28. To what extent do Christians actually disagree about what Christian ethics are?

29. "Christian moral principles are not self-evident." Discuss.

Christian Moral Action

30. "Using the will of God as a guide for moral behaviour is impractical, as in most circumstances it is impossible to know what god wants us to do." Discuss.

31. To what extent, if at all, does the theology of Bonhoeffer have relevance for Christians today?

32. "Bonhoeffer's most important teaching is on leadership." Discuss.

33. "Christian ethics means being obedient to god's will." Discuss.

34. To what extent was Bonhoeffer's religious community at Finkenwalde successful?

Pluralism

35. "A theologically pluralist approach significantly undermines the central doctrines of Christianity." Discuss.

36. To what extent can non-Christians who live morally good lives and genuinely seek God be considered to be 'anonymous Christians'?

37. Critically assess the view that only Christianity offers the means of salvation

38. "Christianity is one of many ways to salvation." Discuss.

Pluralism – Secular

39. To what extent should Christians seek to convert others to Christianity at every opportunity?

40. "Inter-faith dialogue is of little practical use." Discuss.

41. To what extent does scriptural reasoning relativise religious beliefs?

42. "Converting people of no faith should be equally important to a Christian as converting people of non-Christian faith." Discuss.

Pluralism – Religious

43. To what extent should Christians seek to convert others to Christianity at every opportunity?

44. "Inter-faith dialogue is of little practical use." Discuss.

45. To what extent does scriptural reasoning relativise religious beliefs?

46. "Converting people of no faith should be equally important to a Christian as converting people of non-Christian faith." Discuss.

47. Secularism – Christianity Effects

48. "Christianity has a negative impact on society." Discuss.

49. To what extent are Christian values more than just basic human values?

50. "Christianity should play no part in public life." Discuss.

51. Critically assess the claims that God is an illusion and the result of wish fulfilment.

Liberation Theology

52. To what extent should Christianity engage with atheist secular ideologies?

53. "Liberation theology has not engaged with Marxism fully enough." Discuss.

54. Critically assess the claim that Christianity has tackled social issues more effectively than Marxism.

55. Critically assess the relationship of liberation theology and Marx with particular reference to liberation theology use of Marx to analyse social sin.

Gender & Society

56. Christians should resist current secular views of gender" Discuss

57. Evaluate the view that secular views of gender equality have undermined Christian gender roles

58. "Motherhood liberates rather than restricts". Discuss

59. Critically evaluate the view that idea of family is entirely culturally determined.

60. "Christianity follows where culture leads". Discuss

Gender & Theology

61. 'A male saviour cannot save'. Discuss with reference to the theologies of Rosemary Ruether and Mary Daly.

62. "If God is male the male is God'. Discuss

63. Critically contrast the theologies of Ruether and Daly.

64. "The Church is irredeemably patriarchal'. Discuss

65. "God is genderless, and so the idea of the Father-God is idolatry". Discuss

66. "Only a spirituality of women can save the planet from environmental degradation and war'. Discuss

What the Mark Scheme Says - Specimen Paper 2016

Examiners mark against suggested indicative content such as the suggestions on one of the questions "Hell is an idea, not a place', below. The examiners report (published sometime in the autumn) gives us further clues as to which interpretations the examiner finds acceptable and which will be rejected. Usually interpretations allowable and credited are wider than we think. It's for us to impose interpretation on the question and not to be too surprised if our friends come up with a different interpretation. After all, this is philosophy and a reading which is justified by the form of words in the exam question is perfectly okay even if it takes knowledge from widely varying parts of the specification (and indeed knowledge of sources that no-one and no textbook has mentioned except you are perfectly justifiable if they establish a philosophical case which answers the question in front of you).

Here I comment on one mark scheme and suggestions of indicative content. My comments are in italics, and I am trying to bring out the fact that there are many ways of getting an A* in this paper and these are examiner guidelines only that are published.

'Hell is an idea not a place.' Discuss.

The following is a description of possible content only; all legitimate answers and approaches must be credited appropriately. Learners are expected to make use of scholarly views, academic approaches and sources of wisdom and authority to support their argument.

Notice how the examiner repeatedly stresses this point. Whether all examiners have the knowledge expertise to mark fairly when questions may be answered in so many different ways, is of course open to doubt. If you're uncertain whether you've been marked and graded fairly you should always appeal, but also make sure every year you get hold of the photocopied script to show your teacher (and even send to me for comment), as the boards are reluctant to admit to mistakes in marking and OFQUAL is trying to encourage a reduction in the number of appeals.

AO1 Candidates demonstrate knowledge and understanding and may use some of the following ideas about hell:

Notice again how open-ended this is as there are several ideas about hell even in the Bible itself and many different interpretations in history. In medieval times if you look at the paintings by Hieronymous Bosch you will see tortured bodies being pitch-forked into a burning pit by horned devils. Jesus' words on Gehenna in Matthew 25 (a set text), the fiery rubbish tip outside Jerusalem, could of course be pictorial language.

the traditional idea that hell is punishment after death for those who have committed moral sins or have sinned without remorse

It would be good to quote someone here such as Augustine or Aquinas as 'traditional view' is somewhat vague.

in Matthew 25:31-46 (set text) hell (gehenna or hades) is described as a place of fire where there is wailing and gnashing of teeth, which might be taken as a literal depiction of hell, or interpreted differently as symbolic, these interpretations will cause different beliefs and teaching regarding hell

Remember my integrating principle 2 in an earlier chapter, of hermeneutics? It would be more scholarly to contrast a liberation theologian's view of hell with a conservative evangelical view (take someone like CS Lewis or John Stott). Also, why not bring in historic doctrinal statements such as the Westminster confession? Try researching different interpretations of Matthew 25.How do these change according to the historical period or culture?

the wicked will be sent to hell, 'the outer darkness' (Matthew 25:41), and good to 'eternal life' (Matthew 25:46); different interpretations of the text lead to different beliefs about hell in Revelation 20:15 hell is depicted as a lake of fire, where those whose name is not written in the book of life are cast; it is also a place of sulphur (14:10, 19:20) and everlasting torment (20:10)); many Christians take this literally, although in contemporary Christianity symbolic interpretations of these images are commonplace. These interpretations will cause different beliefs and teaching regarding hell.

Again the key issue, unstated, is hermeneutics - how and why we interpret different Bible passages in different ways. What principles of interpretation do we apply? This issue underlies any attempt to interpret Scripture and if we ignore it we come up with a thin, GCSE style answer. To me it's the black hole at the heart of the specification - a failure to make any allusion to issues of interpretation which nonetheless lurk as a philosophical question underlying debates about pluralism, revealed knowledge of God, and differences between Protestant and Catholic views on things like purgatory (a Catholic doctrine, not Protestant). Is gehenna an allusion to purgatory? Or everlasting damnation? Moreover, Matthew 25 is fundamentally incompatible with the Protestant reformation view of justification by faith as it implies justification by works (what we do to the least of these…).

hell as a place is developed through the writings of Augustine and especially Dante with his elaborate depiction of the nine circles of hell from limbo to eternal damnation

Also discussed by most of the Church Fathers from Irenaeus to Boethius to Aquinas.

the Catholic Church's description of hell is the 'eternal separation from God, in whom alone man can possess the life and happiness for which he was created and for which he longs', also 'a state of definitive self-exclusion from communion with God and the blessed' which some Catholics use to downplay the physical properties of hell. Contemporary evangelical and conservative Christian teaching stresses the existence of hell especially when exhorting moral purity and preparation for Christ's second coming.

Yet neither Catholic nor evangelical think hell is a physical place with fire. In other words the idea of separation - a spiritual state of permanent non-being if you like, has replaced medieval views of a physical place of fire and torment - arguably because of the influence of the Enlightenment and changes in our view of the Universe. Heaven is no longer 'up there' and hell 'down there'.

secular interpretations of religion have suggested that hell is a concept that has been invented (along with heaven) to control people or that has come from neurosis; these ideas will create very different beliefs and teachings about hell from those put forward by religious thinkers

This is a particular reference to Freud and the Future if an Illusion, which is a set text in the ChristianThought secularism section which overlaps here.

AO2 Candidates may demonstrate evaluation and analysis through the use of some of the following arguments:

some candidates might argue that hell is a place because:

- the New Testament suggests that the Kingdom of God is a perfect transformed state which rewards the good, so hell must be a corresponding state which punishes the wicked

- the descriptions of torment and suffering in the New Testament only make sense if they are actual physical states

Fairly generalised vagueness here in the examiner's comments. It is possible to argue that heaven is a spiritual condition which begins with belief in God - which is the argument in the Greek influenced gospel of John. Eternal life starts here on earth and simply continues after death. Mark's gospel may be speaking of a transformed eschatological state of the world after judgement day. You need to make some nuanced sense of these bigger issues.

- if hell is an embodied state, because body and soul are not in harmony, then it must be a place or else there would be not be actual infliction of physical pain on the body

Is this meant to be a psychological explanation of hell? If so it sounds Freudian to me, and we might invoke some of the liberal theologians such as Hans Kung to try and make sense of this psych-spiritual condition.

I would prefer to look at the question of hell as an issue of hermeneutics. Some evangelicals may still argue for a physical place of torment and a physical resurrection into physical paradise which is made from of the present earth, without imperfections and sin. In this way hell has to be linked to the doctrine of the second coming of Christ. We need to look again at the evangelical hermeneutic of Scripture.

some candidates might argue that hell is not a place because:

- if Jesus' teaching on the Kingdom of God referred to God's kingly rule or reign then hell (and heaven) are not places but the experience of being alienated from his presence

Again, this view emerges form the Greek-inspired gospel of John, written late, in AD90.

- if Jesus taught that the Kingdom of God is an inner moral and spiritual kingdom, then hell is not a place but a description of human life without God's love

- if the images of hell in Matthew's Gospel are interpreted as metaphors of those who have not repented, then hell is not literally a place but an idea

- the Sheep and Goats parable in Matthew 25: 31-46 (set text) is not so much about future judgement at the end of time but a warning about moral behaviour: the references to hell and heaven are not to places but the qualities of just and unjust people in society as God is good and loving, then he would not create a physical state of hell; hell is better expressed as a state of alienation from God and part of the process of spiritual development

- some candidates may combine these views and consider that although hell may not be a place, it must be more than an idea in order to have the psychological power to show what it means to be truly alienated from God's love.

I would encourage you to contrast the two concepts 'idea' and 'place' and consider whether the question doesn't close off the options. Perhaps hell is neither, but an experience of suffering which we all endure on earth when we go against the divine ordination of the good life. Not a place, not an idea, but an experience. The question itself is set up as an either/or fallacy. Neither views are necessarily correct and there is a third option. Remember to attack the question if you wish to get an A*.

How to Handle Questions with Scripture References

You can see from the table below that Scripture references appear in two out of three papers either in the specification itself, or in suggested reading. The suggested reading references I have put in brackets because these cannot appear in the exam question itself. But it is quite possible that specific references in the specification will appear one day in the actual exam as a question. Presently I will make a list of suggested possible questions, but meantime, let's consider how many references there are and in which papers they are likely to appear.

Philosophy of Religion	Ethics	Christian Thought
(Ontological argument: Psalm 14:1)		(Human Nature: Romans 7:15–20)
(Religious experience Acts 9.4–8, 22.6–10, 26)		**Death and the Afterlife: Matthew 25:31–46** (Revelation 20: 2–6, 7–15 and 21:1–8)
(Problem of evil: Genesis 2:4–25, 3:1–24 Romans 5:12–13)		(Knowledge of God: Romans 1:18–21 Acts 17:16–34)

(Nature of God: Matthew 19:23-26)		**Person of Christ:** **Mark 6:47–52 & John 9:1–41** **Matthew 5:17–48 & Luke** **15:11–32** **Mark 5:24–34 & Luke 10:25–** **37**
		(Christian Moral Principles Exodus 20:1–17 1 Corinthians 13:1–7)
		(Christian Moral Action: Romans 13:1–7 Luke 10:38–42)
		Gender and Society: **Ephesians 5:22–33**
		(Gender and Theology: Luke 24:9–12 Acts 16:13–15)

To do this kind of analysis is quite simple and the results here are surprising. There isn't a single mention of a Bible passage in the Ethics paper H573/2. No mention of the parable of the Good Samaritan and its link to situation ethics. No mention of passages such as Psalm 86 under sanctity of human life and euthanasia. Not even a mention of Paul's version of natural law in Romans 2, or conscience which some feel was introduced into the world as a concept by Paul, see again Romans, this time chapter 1. It's as if the ethics specification was written by an atheist (maybe it was). Of course it doesn't stop you citing and discussing passages such as these.

Secondly, we can note that only in the Christian Thought paper can you expect to get a bible passage actually mentioned in the exam question (because it's in the actual specification, not the suggested reading which I have placed in brackets). I pick the anticipated passages out in bold. There could be questions from Death and the Afterlife, Person of Christ, and Gender and Society which mention a specific bible passage.

What might these questions look like?

With reference to the parable of the Sheep and the Goats (Matthew 25:31-46) assess the view that in Christianity people will be condemned to hell for their actions.

Using Matthew 25:31-46, critically assess the evidence that Christians believe hell to be a physical place.

With reference to Mark 6:47-52 and John 9:1-41, what grounds are there for arguing Jesus thought of himself as a divinely-anointed Messiah?

"Jesus was just a teacher of wisdom". Discuss, with reference to Matthew 5:17-48.

"Jesus Christ was a revolutionary liberator". Assess this view with reference to Mark 5:24-34.

Evaluate the view that Paul's teachings are the origin of sexism, with reference to Ephesians 5:22-33.

Let's be clear: all these are quite fair and legitimate questions. Let's also be clear: few students are equipped to handle this sort of question. The reason is this, returning to my second integrating principle of hermeneutics, there is no guidance in the specification about how to interpret scripture and evaluate big questions arising out of so-called literal readings of these chapters. So here are some suggestions.

1. Link these passages to religious pluralism and try to understand the mindset of the literalist or fundamentalist (sometimes misleadingly called bible-believing) interpretation which is exemplified by

statements such as the Chicago Declaration on Biblical Inerrancy of 1978. Then contrast this with the liberal interpretations which might be inspired by Bultmann on myth or Hick on universal pluralism. You will see how a variety of readings come out of two different philosophical positions.

2. Try to do a proper case study on these passages and see how they are interpreted by the eras of history I mentioned under integrating principle 1 in an earlier chapter. So take Augustine's reading, Aquinas' reading, Calvin's reading, and compare these to the feminist readings of the same passage (I'm thinking here of Ephesians) or liberationist readings of Matthew 25. By the way, in ten years worshipping in various evangelical churches I never once heard a sermon on Matthew 25 because it appears to teach an evangelical heresy: that we are justified (saved) according to our works, not by our faith. Calvin's commentary is interesting here., which I've placed on the peped website (section on Death and the Afterlife)

3. Always place Scripture in context. The New Testament needs to be interpreted in the context of the Old Testament, and one verse in the New Testament in the context of the whole book in which it comes. I know it sounds like hard work, but you really need to examine the theology of Matthew to understand Matthew 25, and Paul's whole theology of personhood to understand Ephesians 5. That's if you want to get an A grade on this sort of questions. Finally the whole Bible needs to be placed in the context of its time. If you want to understand the times of Jesus the best summary I have read is in Ched Myers' book, Binding the Strong Man, a Political Reading of Mark, chapter 1. This book is a very useful bridge, too, to liberation theology.

How Might We Handle Ephesians 5?

This book is not a textbook, but because textbooks gloss over this whole issue of hermeneutics and how we read texts, and how texts are read by different cultures, Let me illustrate from Ephesians 5 how the issues arise, and what we might say that isn't naive over-generalisation. There is a problem, however, on a superficial reading, Ephesians 5 does appear to be offensive and sexist to the modern reader:

Wives, submit yourselves to your own husbands as you do to the Lord. For the husband is the head of the wife as Christ is the head of the church, his body, of which he is the Saviour. Now as the church submits to Christ, so also wives should submit to their husbands in everything. (Ephesians 5:22-24)

First of all there is the issue of the text itself. The earliest manuscript we have of Paul's letter is the Codex Vaticanus (dated 325 AD), does not contain the key word 'submit' in Ephesians 5:22 'wives, submit to your husbands as to the Lord'. Was this key verse therefore a later addition, placed there by church authorities worried about the radicalness of some of Paul's statements? There would also seem to be a 'controlling thought' in this passage - 'submit yourselves to one another out of reverence to Christ' (Ephesians 5:21), which implies a mutual submission to each other in the spirit of sacrificial love, rather than the inferiority of women. It is the agape of situation ethics that seems to be in control here.

Secondly, notice that this verse (in its later version) fundamentally contradicts Paul's teaching in Galatians: "now therefore, there is neither Jew nor Greek, slave nor free, male nor female, we are all one In Christ Jesus" (Galatians 3:28). There are few more revolutionary statements in the Bible about gender equality than this one. So which is the real Paul? And how does this square with Jesus' very revolutionary attitude to women, shown, for example, in Mark 5 when he addresses the bleeding woman who had just polluted him by touching his cloak: "daughter, go in peace, your faith has made you well". The outcast becomes Jesus' daughter and inner member of the family. The Kingdom is dawning in a new set of relationships, including gender relationships.

As we interpret the Bible we have to attempt to reconcile supposedly contradictory statements, otherwise we do neither Paul nor Jesus justice.

Finally, we need to realise that the interpretations given to this passage by, for example, Augustine, are not 'pure' interpretations, but in his case, clouded by neo-Platonic ideas including those of the fundamental irrationality and inferiority of women. Have modern evangelical interpretations of women's issues simply inherited uncritically Augustine's distortion? Here's what Augustine says, and notice the body/soul dualism here which is transposed onto male/female gender differences:

The apostle puts flesh for woman; because, when she was made of his rib, Adam said, "This is now bone of my bone, and flesh of my flesh." And the apostle says, "He that loves his wife loves himself; for no one ever hated his own flesh." Flesh, then, is put for woman, in the same manner that spirit is sometimes put for husband. Why? Because the one rules, the other is ruled; the one ought to command, the other to serve. For where the flesh commands and the spirit serves, the house is turned the wrong way round. What can be worse than a house where the woman has the mastery over the man? But that house is rightly ordered where the man commands and the woman obeys. In like manner that man is rightly ordered where the spirit commands and the flesh serves. (Augustine, On John Tractate 2, § 14)

Notice that Augustine argues that just as the spirit is superior to the body, so the husband, even though he is flesh, is superior to the wife. It's a strange and twisted piece of logic but the end result is Augustine's conclusion: a house is rightly ordered where a man commands and a woman obeys.

What has happened here is that neo-Platonic categories and dualisms have filtered Augustine's interpretation, just as prejudices about women pre-filter (arguably) how evangelical Christians seem to read the Bible. Or so would be my argument, the point being, we need to discuss how these texts are interpreted and consider whether the superficial interpretation, or the historical one of Augustine quoted above, is actually correct. And what principles drive their sometimes very different interpretations?

Our conclusion is that the traditional reading is actually a patriarchal reading of Ephesians which rejects the radical, liberating idea of mutual submission in Christian marriage. It insists that just as Jesus was the Lord and Master of the church, so too must a husband be lord and master of his wife. In other words, according to patriarchal theology, it is the "lordship" of Jesus that husbands are told to imitate in marriage.

But is this the thrust of Paul's argument? It would seem not: his argument is based on the equality principle of considering one another's interests above your own, the agape principle in Christ's example of outpouring and giving love. It's easy to miss this fundamental point if you selectively quote Ephesians 5:22, a text that may well be a later insertion by the church. These are the issues underlying the concept of the 'two horizons of hermeneutics' (see integrating principle 2 in an earlier chapter).

:

Some Revision Tips for A Grade

1. REVISION TIP - Make up your own exam questions using the type of wording mentioned in the previous chapter, for areas that the examiner has not yet asked about. You can use oft-repeated phrases like "issues surrounding". Remember that, with applied ethical questions, specific theories are going to be linked to certain areas: natural law and situation ethics to euthanasia issues, Kant and utilitarian ethics to business ethics, and any of these four to sexual ethics. We need to pay close attention to unpacking the 'issues surrounding' these applied areas. I would encourage you to have three pre-prepared issues with contrasting viewpoints and scholars also pre-prepared.

2. REVISION TIP - Prepare a grid with the issues on one axis and the major theories on the other. Fill in the squares with some key points, for example, on how a Kantian interprets the absolute categoricals with respect to business ethics, or using the second formulation of the Categorical Imperative: "never use people just as a means to an end, but always, also as an end in themselves", how this applies to how you treat stakeholders. You can then compare this with a utilitarian view of business ethics, perhaps grounding it in some case studies

3. REVISION TIP- One minute debates are useful to encourage quick-thinking analysis. The teacher arranges chairs or desks in a circle with some students inside and some outside. The teacher then pre-prepares (or gets the class to pre-prepare) some "Discuss"questions. Then the students argue the case, the inner circle taking one view and the outer circle another (for and against the proposition). After one minute the whistle blows and the inner circle moves on one place. If you're stuck for questions, use my lists

here.

When the debate has been had four or five times, a plenary session can be held where we construct together the strongest case on either side. Then the students can vote on which side they would like to prepare, and write a paragraph summarising the viewpoint. Finally each student can be asked to write a paragraph justifying their view - which must have reasons to back the view up. A prize could awarded for the most analytical answer.

4. REVISION TIP: Use real examples from the newspaper which are provided by the peped site or your own reading or your own research. There are some good films based on real life events, such as Erin Brokovitch on business ethics, and the Constant Gardener. Recent cases in business ethics include Glencore and Trafigura. Try to establish the motive of managers in these cases, and whether a study of ethical theories would have helped them.

5. REVISION TIP: try writing your own suggested indicative content (like the OCR specimen paper example above from 2016) and then try criticising it or elaborating on it as a group. the examiner's comments (see page 151) are often too vague and generalised as they stand and need a much more detailed treatment. Also, try imposing one of the integrating principles I mentioned in an earlier chapter onto any exam question. What does hell say about God and about being human? Is hell really a projection of our ideas of retributive justice onto the idea of God?

6. REVISION TIP - try writing your own exam questions with different trigger words (command words like 'to what extent') in them. Practise the opening paragraph with different trigger words but essentially the same question. How does the feel of the paragraph change when the trigger word changes? Perhaps sometimes not very much (discuss versus assess, is there much difference?). 'To what extent' does need more careful consideration, I think. The

more your practise writing against the clock (ie a forty minute sustained period for a full essay, and maybe five minutes for an opening paragraph) the better equipped you will be on the day.

It's a persistent complaint of examiners that even good students haven't the skill to deliver a balanced analysis and evaluation in forty minutes. Students are poorly taught on this point, or under-practised. Probably this, together with a failure to treat the question on its merits, are two main reason why students fall off an A grade, and so potentially lose a University offer.

Spot the Gaps in Past Questions

Where one area is missed out in one paper it is usually examined in some form in the next paper set. A thorough analysis of the specification also tells us that some themes in the specification have never been examined. This makes them more likely to come up, the longer they stay absent. There are also particular slants on a familiar topic area which have never been examined.

Students often ask me if they can safely leave a topic area out altogether (the least favourite one being Meta-ethics in ethics papers for example). The answer is probably and only with great reservations, "yes" to this, as long as the strategies for handling any topic area suggested in this book are followed. Leave out meta-ethics (for example) and you will still have three questions to choose from out of four. Trouble comes, however, when one of these is a very tricky question on your favourite area - one with a twist you're not expecting.

Having said that: if you can master, say, meta-ethics, the questions are really quite predictable, and usually revolve around a core issue - which theory best makes sense of ethical statements. You can attack emotivism fairly hard as few people these days see much validity in AJ Ayer's view, whereas a theory like Prescriptivism (which is no longer in the new specification, but may be introduced if you wish to evaluate Ayer) would seem to be truer to how we use moral language.

Remember too that naturalism (the objective basis for ethical statements) has made a comeback and so an answer defending naturalism against the naturalistic fallacy attack makes for an interesting essay, which will stand out in this less popular topic area.

Philosophy of Religion

	2017 AS	2018 AS	2018 A Level
Plato and Aristotle		2. Critically assess Aristotle's understanding of the world.	
Mind body and Soul	1. 'There is no such thing as a soul.' Discuss.		
A Priori Arguments		3. Examine the success of Kant's criticisms to the Ontological Argument.	
A Posteriori Arguments	3. To what extent does Aquinas' cosmological argument successfully reach the conclusion that there is a transcendent creator?		2. To what extent does Hume successfully argue that observation does not prove the existence of God?
Religious Experience		1. Conversion experiences do not provide basis for a belief in God.	4. 'Corporate religious experiences are less reliable than individual religious experience.' Discuss.

Problem of Evil	2. Assess the claim that natural evil has a purpose.		
Nature of God			3. Assess Boethius' view that divine eternity does not limit human free will.
Religious Language – Classic			1. 'The best approach to understanding religious language is through the Cataphatic Way.' Discuss.
Religious Language – Logical Positivism			

Ethics

	2017 AS	2018 AS	2018 A Level
Natural Law	1. To what extent does Natural Law provide a helpful method of moral decision making?		Assess the view that Natural Law is of no help with regard to the issue of euthanasia.

Situation Ethics		2. 'The concept of agape gives no help at all in moral decision-making.' Discuss.	
Kantian Ethics	2. 'Kantian ethics is too abstract to be useful in practical moral decision-making.		Kantian ethics provide the best approach to business ethics.' Discuss.
Utilitarianism		3. Critically assess the view that Utilitarianism provides a helpful way to make moral decisions.	
Euthanasia		1. Voluntary Euthanasia is always morally acceptable.	Assess the view that Natural Law is of no help with regard to the issue of euthanasia.
Business Ethics	3. 'The only purpose of a business is to make profit.' Discuss.		Kantian ethics provide the best approach to business ethics.' Discuss.
Meta Ethics			"Good" is meaningful." Discuss.
Conscience			Evaluate Aquinas' theological approach to conscience.
Sexual Ethics			

Developments in Christian Thought

	2017 AS	2018 AS	2018 A Level
Augustine		1. Critically assess the significance of Augustine's teaching on human relationships before the Fall.	
Death and the Afterlife	1. Critically assess the view that in Christian teaching all people will be saved.		
Knowledge of God		3. To what extent is faith the only means of knowing God?	
Person of Jesus Christ	2. 'Jesus' teaching was only about becoming a moral person.' Discuss.		To what extent was Jesus merely a political liberator?
Christian Moral Principles		2. 'The most important source for Christian ethics is Church teaching.' Discuss.	

Christian Moral Action	3. To what extent was Dietrich Bonhoeffer justified in his teaching on civil disobedience?		Bonhoeffer's theology is still relevant today.' Discuss.
Religious Plurialism			
Gender			Assess the view that Mary Daly's theology proves that Christianity is sexist.
Secularism and Liberation Theology			Secularism does not pose a threat to Christianity.' Discuss.

What the Examiner Says

Every year the examiner produces a report on student answers available on the OCR website. It is possible to extract from these general principles what goes wrong when you write essays under exam conditions. Actually the same points are made over and over again, as if no-one ever reads the reports and if they do, fail to learn from them. I have summarised here the main points the examiner makes from the OCR old Specification (before 2016) as I believe these still remain valid (and we don't have any examiners reports as I write this, to do an analysis for the new specification), and then I suggest twelve things to practise to try and eliminate these errors.

Answer the question

It sounds an obvious point, but nearly every year the examiner complains that students are deviating off the question, either because they have learned a pre-prepared answer, or because they have more knowledge on another (perhaps related) area and so feel compelled to prove it.

Enormous efforts are made for little credit as this comment in January 2011 indicates:

"An examination at this level is not primarily a test of what candidates know, but rather of how well they can respond to the question. Some candidates wrote at enormous length, covering every theory they could remember, but often without demonstrating how these might be remotely relevant".

As another example, here's a comment praising relevance from a recent report:

"Good candidates kept the question in mind throughout", (Jan 2012 AS Ethics Q4b)

You will not achieve an A grade if you don't answer the exact question set.

When you go into an exam, take a highlighter pen and highlight the key words and phrases. Hopefully, if you study this book carefully, you will understand what sort of command words (like 'Explain") to expect, and indeed, what kind of questions, as the examiner tends to repeat key phrases in different questions. A comment like the one below is fairly typical:

"Generally, candidates fared well provided they answered the question which had been set and not the one they hoped would be set. Candidates need to be reminded to read the question and then answer the question". (June 2012)

▸ Practise: making a reference to the question in every paragraph you write

Know your key terms throughly

In a previous chapter I listed the technical vocabulary in different areas of the syllabus. This creates a minimal list of technical terms you must thoroughly understand and know. There is no excuse for entering an exam in a state of muddle over the distinction between a priori and a posteriori. Here are two comments from recent examiner's reports.

"Words which seemed to have been ignored (or misunderstood) are 'universe', 'inconsistent' and 'biblical'," (Jan 2012 AS Philosophy) *"Significant numbers seemed unaware that a predicate is part of a sentence and is not a quality of a thing".* (June 2012 AS Philosophy)

Then in a longer extract, the examiner reiterates this point:

"Unfortunately, there are still candidates who attempt this examination with insecure knowledge of basic philosophical concepts and terminology. Many remain unaware of the correct meaning of terms such as 'empirical', 'logical ', 'refute', 'metaphysical', 'a priori' or 'a posteriori'. Especially common errors were 'analytical' for 'analytic' – especially and 'scientifical' for 'scientific'. This subject presupposes familiarity with basic philosophical notions and some candidates have paid too little attention to these".

And again, of the old A2 Philosophy of Religion specification, the examiner repeats the criticism that key terms are not properly understood. For example:

A particular problem for many was inadequate grasp of the grammar of philosophy, with terms such as 'prove' used as a synonym for 'argue'. Some would say of each thinker cited that he had 'proved' his view, even when it was controversial or opposed by other alleged 'proofs'; 'refute' used to mean 'deny'; a priori often mistakenly used for 'innate'; a posteriori, 'analytic' and 'metaphysical' were commonly misunderstood. This is an examination in Philosophy of Religion, and understanding the conventions of the subject is as significant as understanding correct notation in Mathematics. Some candidates attempted, normally unsuccessfully, to answer philosophical questions with theological or scriptural assertions, (Jan 2012 A2 Philosophy of Religion).

▸ Practise: learning key definitions off by heart, then using them in a careful, precise and nuanced way.

Reflect, don't just memorise

"Some candidates appeared to have attempted to learn theories, leading to less successful responses: more able responses showed evidence of reflection on theories, with the best showing the benefits of original thought. It cannot be too often stressed that examiners – and the nature of the subject – expect candidates to demonstrate that they have considered and reflected on ideas and not merely learned them". (AS Philosophy Jan 2012).

How do we "reflect on theories"? My argument in this book is that we reflect on theories by not just learning key points off by heart, but also by understanding (and being prepared to challenge) key **assumptions** the theory makes and reflecting carefully on the **worldview** the theory comes out of. We then practise applying the key **principles** suggested by a theory to a particular issue (preferably using our own examples to ground the explanation).

▶ Practise reflective writing by peer group comparison and using examples of good practice on the peped website.

Show higher order skills

"Despite good AO1 performance, AO2 skills were often lacking. It continues to be the characteristic of many candidates to believe that just because a number of philosophers have criticised a theory, it must be wrong, and when evaluating a question, you simply need to count the philosophers who make points on each side of the argument and see which side has more in it", (June 2012 examiners' report).

What are these AO1 and AO2 skills? In general terms these "descriptors", as they are called, can be expressed thus for a full GCE A level (in both a whole essay is assessed according to these in the new specification).

AO1: you must select and demonstrate clearly relevant knowledge and understanding through the use of evidence, examples and correct language and terminology appropriate to Ethics, Christian Thought and Philosophy of Religion.

For top marks (out of 24 maximum for GCE A level AO2) you must show:

An excellent demonstration of analysis and evaluation in response to the question:

- *excellent, clear and successful argument*

- *confident and insightful critical analysis and detailed evaluation of the issue*

- *views skilfully and clearly stated, coherently developed and justified*

- *answers the question set precisely throughout*

- *thorough, accurate and precise use of technical terms and vocabulary in context*

- *extensive range of scholarly views, academic approaches and sources of wisdom and authority used to support analysis and evaluation*

Assessment of Extended Response: There is an excellent line of reasoning, well-developed and sustained, which is coherent, relevant and logically structured.

▸ Practise: reading the list of AO2 skills before you start your essay, and re-read after you've finished

Argue, don't assert

It's worth reflecting long and hard on the longer quotes from examiner's reports below:

"A statement of a viewpoint is not an argument, and argument by assertion is inappropriate in philosophical writing. Many responses simply presented alternative viewpoints but made no attempt to use these to work to their own conclusions. Candidates would benefit from thinking through the implications of the descriptors in the published levels of response used for marking – these are invaluable for explaining precisely those abilities rewarded by examiners". (Jan 2012 AS Philosophy of Religion)

"It is important that candidates engage with arguments: examiners seek evidence that views have been thoughtfully considered. A list of the arguments of different philosophers does not become a considered argument simply because 'however' is occasionally inserted into a narrative account". (June 2012 AS Philosophy of Religion)

"On occasions, some candidates, who were clearly very able, let themselves down by merely stating the views in detail and failing to deploy them as part of an overall argument". (June 2012 AS Philosophy of Religion Q1a)

"Some candidates struggled with the fundamental skill of constructing arguments"

▶ Practise: constructing arguments using the thesis - argument - conclusion model described in my companion book to this one, How to Write Philosophy Essays.

Illustrate with examples

"Good marks were awarded for candidates who were able to demonstrate control of the material as well as being able to give examples from the biblical text to support their explanations". (June 2012 Q2a)

But make sure the examples are fresh and relevant.

'Some candidates continued to use dubious examples to support their explanations and many not even ethical ones, as well as the usual 'helping an old lady to cross the road' and the 'stealing to feed a starving family', (Jan 2012 AS Ethics).

▶ Practise: finding film extracts, news examples, or incidents in novels that illustrate ethical principles. Watch new films critically

Produce an argument, not a list

It is worth reflecting again on what constitutes an argument. If you have difficulty knowing how to practise forming an argument, I give plenty of examples in my book "How to Write Philosophy Essays". Weaker candidates simply list points, rather than integrate them into a line of reasoning. A grade candidates argue and explain points, showing how they link to assumptions and world-views. Here's a comment that confirms this problem:

"Weaker candidates tended to write as much as they knew without focusing on command words such as 'explain'." (June 2012 AS Ethics)

And on Utilitarianism, there is this comment:

"Weaker responses simply described the differences (between Act and Rule Utilitarianism) without any explanation of the reasons behind them", (Jan 2012 AS Ethics Q1a).

▸ Practise: producing argument plans which sketch out counter-arguments and objections, like the Socratic method

Be aware of the various issues (and applications) within a topic

The examiner stressed in the 2010 June report that "candidates must learn how to apply ethical theories to practical ethical issues. Many candidates do not know how to do so and therefore cannot access the higher marks". Genetic engineering is no longer on the specification - but are we familiar with the varieties of active and passive euthanasia, which still is?

"Unfortunately, many candidates seemed to have only a very basic knowledge of what genetic engineering involved. Many candidates only focused on human genetic engineering without mentioning animals or plants. Some candidates focused entirely on IVF treatment without discussing issues such as genetic selection or testing for disease, resulting in a limited viewpoint." (Jan 2012 AS Ethics Q2b)

An example of a former Ethics candidate praised highly by the examiner involves using an entirely correct, but unusual argument in answer to a question (Jan 2012 Q4) on Natural Law. It depends what you mean by 'absolute' (see the appendix for a definition with three meanings).

"One candidate wrote an excellent response showing that Natural Law can be both absolute and relative". (Jan 2012 report on AS Ethics).

▶ Practise: working out the issues surrounding euthanasia, business ethics and sexual ethics, and then apply moral theories to these issues. Try to extract principles from theories

Find out about modern interpretations

For example, the authorised textbooks make no mention of Alister McGrath's new interpretation of natural theology (relevant to the Knowledge of God section of the Christian Thought specification H573/3). This is big omission, because McGrath is arguing that during the Enlightenment Natural Theology took a fundamental wrong turning in trying to 'prove' God exists, and that this isn't the role of natural theology at all.

Even when the specification doesn't mention them, the examiner clearly likes original, up-to-date comments about ethical theories. One example, which slightly surprised me because it seems to depart from the specification (admittedly old specification, but perhaps even more relevant to the new one), is this comment about modern interpretations of Natural Law theory:

'Many were able to make reference to more modern forms of Natural Law theory as found in Proportionalism. Key features such as the concept of telos, eudaimonia, the Primary and Secondary Precepts, apparent and actual goods and intentions behind actions were often highlighted', (Jan 2012 AS Ethics Q4a).

When I read this it reminded me that I had never taught Bernard Hoose's theory of Proportionalism.

I was encouraged by this comment. The examiner is saying "don't read the syllabus over-narrowly". Why not use Christine Korsgaard (a modern Kantian) or Richard Hare (a twentieth century Utilitarian) to help reflect on these two theories? Here's another:

"The best answers, of which there were few, were able to use the work of Norman Malcolm or Alvin Plantinga to critically attack Kant's work through the notion of God's unlimited nature or maximal greatness to support Anselm's claim that God is a special case." *(June 2012 AS Philosophy Q1b)*

▸ Practise: finding modern scholars who represent different viewpoints on old questions or theories, and who aren't mentioned in textbooks (which often have a very limited and subjective selection of philosophers additional to the specification).

Consult the peped website for extracts listed by section which cover the suggested reading in the specification, and represent a breadth of scholarly views that the assessment criteria demand.

My final advice: don't over-rely on textbooks, which have done their own selection and often don't have space to explain the new ideas they introduce properly. Follow your own curiosity and those leads which open up to you, research, compare, pursue understanding, not rote-learning, and you will get much closer to an A*.

References

Ahluwahlia L. and Bowie R. Oxford A Level Religious Studies for OCR (OUP, 2017)

Baron P. Ethics, A Study Guide (Peped, 2018)

Baron P. How to Write Philosophical Essays (Peped, 2016)

Berger, P. A Rumour of Angels (Anchor, 1970)

Capone A. Philosophy of Religion: A Study Guide (Peped, 2018)

Dunsmore, D. & Baron P. Christian Thought, A Study Guide (Peped, 2018)

Dawkins, R. The God Delusion (Black Swan, 2016)

Freud S. The Future of an Illusion (Penguin, 2008)

Myers C. Binding the Strong Man: A Political Reading of Mark's Story of Jesus (Orbis, 2008)

Thiselton A. The Two Horizons (Eerdmans, 1996)

Vermes G. The Religion of Jesus the Jew (SCM, 2011)

Wilcockson M. and Wilkerson M. OCR Religious Studies, Year 1 and 2 (Hodder 2017)

Wilcockson, M. Christian Theology (Hodder, 2009)

Appendix of Technical Terms

Here is my own set of definitions of every technical term mentioned in the OCR specification H573/1/2/3.

a posteriori - means 'after experience', or 'from observation'. A posteriori arguments include the teleological argument, and the ethical theory of natural law, which derives goodness from observed rational tendencies God has designed into us.

a priori - means 'before experience". A priori arguments proceed by logical deduction, for example the ontological argument for God's existence, or Kant's theory of ethics.

absolutism - 'absolute' means one of three things - a theory is universal (applies to everyone) or that a principle is non-negotiable (unchanging) or that it is objective - tested empirically so beyond dispute.

act utilitarianism - the utility of an act is its ability to maximise happiness and minimise pain - tested by applying the greatest happiness principle to likely consequences of a single action.

agape - one of the four loves of Greek ethics, meaning unconditional commitment to friend and stranger, as in Jesus' saying 'greater agape has no-one than this, that a person lay down his life for his friends" (John 15:13). It is both the foundation principle of situation ethics, and a vital issue in Christian moral principles (Christian Thought).

analogy of attribution - Aquinas' view that you can say God is like blazing sun (attribute of purity and light). But it's an analogy because there isn't a precise one for one likeness between God and the attribute of light. As God is the cause of all good things, God's attributes are simply on a higher level to our own. Hick gave examples of 'upwards' analogy of attribution, such as speaking of a dog's faithfulness as analogical to the faithfulness of God.

anaphatic or apophatic way - a philosophical approach to theology which asserts that no finite concepts or attributes can be adequately used of God, but only negative terms, such as immortal, immutable or invisible. Apophasis means 'denial, negation' and so 'apophatic' is another word for anaphatic.

analogy of proper proportion - A plant has a life, a human has life, God has life - there is a proportionate relationship between each life mentioned in the list, with God's being the greatest and the plants being on a proportionately lower level.

attributes - (divine) qualities of God's character such as omnibenevolence, omnipotence and omniscience. Notice these can be expressed positively as in the via positiva or negatively as in the via negativa (God is immortal, so not mortal, invisible, so not visible).

categorical imperative - A term Kant employs to express an unconditional, absolute maxim or command - an imperative like 'never lie!'

category error - applying a category from one form of life to another which it cannot refer to - such as 'what colour is the wind?" The wind never has a colour.

cognitive approaches to language - an imposition on the debate on religious and ethical language from the Enlightenment concern for verification and 'meaningfulness' - cognitive approaches examine the truth value of statements according to their verifiability (testability by experience). So 'examination of the truth-aptness of statements'.

conscientia - Aquinas' one of two words for conscience, meaning 'reason making right decisions', he other being 'synderesis', for example, judging what to do in natural law theory when two goods conflict and we need to judge how to apply the principle of double effect means applying the judgement of reason.

corporate social responsibility - a theory developed by Edward Freeman which states that corporations should take responsibility for the consequences of their actions for all stakeholders and for the environment, and not just shareholders.

cosmological - to do with first causes - the cosmological argument is concerned to establish God as first cause of everything (as first muted by Aristotle's prime mover).

divine law - one of the four laws of natural law ethics, sees the inaccessible eternal law revealed to us in two ways by God - by divine law (the Bible) and natural law (morality). Echoes here of Plato's Forms of the good and Kant's noumenal (inaccessible) realm of reality.

efficient cause - one of Aristotle's four causes which implies the process by which something comes into being - eg the sculptor forms the clay to make his art.

ego - one of Freud's three classifications of the human psyche, the ego is the reality principle which forms as we realise how to present ourselves to the public world, even with the contradictions and conflicts within us.

emotivism - a theory of ethical language developed by AJ Ayer from the logical positivists of the Vienna Circle, which concludes that all ethical statements are simply expressions of emotion and have no factual (cognitive, truth-apt) content.

empiricism - the view that the meaningfulness and truth conditions of experience are required to test our knowledge of reality. Their views affect both issues of language and of testability, but as the empiricist Hume concedes there is a problem in induction - we cannot finally prove the sun will rise tomorrow.

eternal law - one fo the four laws of Aquinas' natural law which refers to the inaccessible mind and purposeful design of God, whose blueprint is only partially revealed to us.

exclusivism - a view in the debate about theological pluralism which states that Jesus is the only 'way, the truth and the life' as in John 14:6.

extramarital sex - sexual relations outside marriage between at least one married person and another (irrespective of gender).

fall - the Fall of humankind in Genesis 3 occurred when Eve disobeyed God by taking the fruit fro the tree of knowledge and giving it to Adam, who disobeys by eating it. In consequence, they are expelled from Eden, Eve gets pain in childbirth and Adam finds weeds growing in the garden as God's curse - also Adam 'has dominion' over Eve and she 'desires him' - Augustine sees this as the moment lust (cupiditas) enters the world.

fallacy -   a mistake in deductive logic when one thing doesn't follow from another. In the naturalistic fallacy (meta-ethics) the fallacy is that we move from is statements to ought statements without supplying an answer to the question - this may be pleasurable, but what exactly makes it good?

falsificationism - conditions by which a proposition may be considered false, for example, the proposition 'the sun will rise tomorrow' can be falsified because the sun may not rise tomorrow.

five ways - the five proofs in Aquinas for the existence of God which include - the unmoved mover, the first cause, the argument from necessity (contingency), the argument from degree, and the argument from ends (the teleological argument). All these are forms of cosmological argument. Richard Dawkins criticisms of Aquinas' argument has been challenged by Keith ward and Alister McGrath.

formal cause - the concept in the mind of the sculptor before he takes the clay (material cause), sculpts (efficient cause) and produces a work of art (final cause). the formal cause of the existence of the universe is part of God's eternal law in natural law ethics.

formula of kingdom of ends - Kant's formal principe, that defines goodness, that we should so act as to imagine ourselves a lawmaker in a kingdom of ends, with the consistent rules that would follow.

formula of law of nature (law) - Kant's formula that we should act according to a maxim which can be willed as a universal law for the whole fo humanity.

formula of the end in itself (ends) - Kant's formula, often misquoted, that we should treat people not simply as a means to an end, but always also as an end in themselves. He never said as Fletcher states - don't treat people as means, but only as ends.

globalisation - the process of opening up global markets and global culture so that people trade, interchange and share products, views, and values freely and without restrictions.

grace - God's generous gifts to humanity of love, sustaining power, and life itself. Jesus is described as 'full of grace and truth' (John 1:14). Closely linked to the character of God int he Old Testament of hesed (Hebrew - steadfast love) and emeth (Hebrew - truth or faithfulness).

hedonic calculus - Bentham's way of calculating the balance of pleasure over pain in an action by seven criteria - things such as intensity, extent and duration of the pleasure.

hypothetical imperative - a command with an 'if' in it - if you are faced with an axe murderer asking after your friend, you should lie (a famous Kantian example). Kant felt morality was based on categorical absolutes, not conditional statements with an 'if' making them relative to circumstances.

id - Freud's term for the part of the psyche which follows the pleasure principle of satisfying needs and desires, typified by the screaming baby.

inclusivism - a term in religious pluralism which means that all ways (religions) lead to God, and no one path excludes others. Hick's universal pluralism is an example.

innate - means 'born with' and so in natural law ethics we are all born with a tendency to do good and avoid evil a kind of inbuilt knowledge called synderesis.

intuitionism - a theory of goodness that holds that we know right and wrong by intuition, a kind of inbuilt perception. GE Moore argues that good is an indefinable, non-reducible, simple property of an action which we just recognise like the colour yellow.

invincible ignorance - ignorance of sin and morality which Aquinas believes gives us an excuse, for example, because we have never heard of Jesus or the Bible.

limited election - the argument that only certain people will be saved - either those predestined (Calvin) or those who have repented and chosen to believe (general Protestant view)

material cause - the stuff something is made of, such as clay in a sculpture.

materialism - a Marxist idea that human beings have been reduced to an object which is in fundamental conflict with other objects, particularly the capitalist against the worker where both are 'objectified'. Also refers more generally to a human desire and obsession to get wealth.

messiah - the 'anointed one', and the hope of Israel that one day 'a son is born, a son is given who shall be called wonderful counsellor, Mighty God, Prince of Peace'. In the Person of Christ section of Christian Thought, the debate about whether Jesus thought himself the special one (Messiah) in a divine sense and what the title 'Son of God' actually meant.

meta-ethics - 'beyond ethics' so the language and meaning of ethical terms, and questions of the foundation of ethics, whether it is naturalistic (something in the world) or non-naturalistic.

metaphysics - beyond physics and so that which is not observable/measurable by science, such as truth, beauty and love (includes God, of course).

mystical experience - experience that cannot be explained by science or medicine, such as the visions of St Teresa of Avila, or Paul's meeting Christ on the road to Damascus in Acts.

natural knowledge - knowledge that can be gained from observing nature. The teleological argument, that God has designed patterns into nature, is an inference from natural knowledge.

natural law - a theory of ethics originating from Aristotle and developed by Aquinas, that human beings have a true rational purpose designed into them, observable a posteriori by the goals we by our nature's pursue. The 'unofficial moral theology of the Catholic Church' (Singer).

natural religion - religion based on reason rather than divine revelation, especially deism which became popular during the Enlightenment.

naturalism - a debate in meta-ethics about the foundation of ethics, whether it exists in the natural world, or as part of our experience (such as pleasure and pain) or whether it's source is a priori (so non-natural, as Kant agues).

nature of attributes of God - attributes of God typically include his omniscience, omnipotence and omnibenevolence (which are linked to his powers) or faithfulness, steadfast-love and generosity (related to his moral character and holiness).

non-cognitive approaches to language - non-cognitive means 'not truth-apt' ie not verifiable by reference to something else such as observation or experience.

normative means of salvation - the ways by which God saves us, where 'normative' means 'those defined as true and accepted'. In Christianity the normative means of salvation is the cross of Christ, by which he paid the price as a ransom for sin (Mark 10:45).

omnibenevolence - all-loving attribute of God

omnipotence - all-powerful attribute of God

omniscience - all-knowing attribute of God

ontological - means 'of the essence' as in the ontological argument for the existence of God which derives from his essence as ever-existing and perfect.

original sin - sin coming from the choice of Adam and Eve in the Garden to disobey God and eat the fruit of the tree of knowledge. Augustine believed this original sin was transmitted ever-after by the male semen. It's a debate in Knowledge of God (Christian Thought) how much we can 'see' God ourselves in nature, and how much original sin permanently blinds us.

personalism - one of the working principles of Situation ethics, meaning 'related to the effect on the individual'. Fletcher argues ethics should be related to individual needs and desires, not imposed as law.

pluralism - means 'many views of truth and goodness'.

positivism - has two meanings, rather different. Fletcher cites positivism as a working principle of situation ethics, meaning 'received by faith and then lived by'. Whereas in logical positivism in meta-ethics and religious language it means 'provable by a principle of verification'.

postulates - things put forward as self-evident, as assumptions, as in Kant's ethical theory which postulates God, immortality and freedom.

pragmatism - one of Fletcher's four working principles in situation ethics, meaning 'practical, based on a real case-by-case approach to ethics'.

primary precept - the five precepts mentioned   by Aquinas as the natural rational goals of human beings (preserve life, order society, worship God, educate and reproduce).

prime mover - an Aristotelean idea that something (God) put the world and cosmos into existence. Became associated with Deism in the eighteenth century as God gets progressively distanced from his creation.

purgatory - a state of being between death and heaven when the soul is purified (or purged) of sin.

ratio - the reason by which we work out the eternal law of God evidenced in experience and by observation. Synderesis in contrast, in natural law ethics, is intuitive reason.

rationalism - a principle of the Enlightenment which has as its motto 'dare to reason' and which exalts reason over metaphysics, and so closely linked to scepticism and secularism (Christian Thought specification). In meta-ethics and religious language debates, influences of rationalists like David Hume cause people to doubt the meaningfulness of religious language.

relativism - means one of three things, relative to consequences, subjective (up to me) or particular to culture (as in 'cultural relativism').

repentance - Greek 'metanoia' means to change direction by renouncing one way and actively embracing another. The first call of Jesus in Mark's gospel is 'repent, for the Kingdom of Heaven is at hand'. In Liberation Theology it means taking up the cause of justice and revolution and overturning social evils.

rule utilitarianism - a   theory of ethics normally attributed to JS Mill which argues that maximising happiness involves the recognition of certain (non-absolute) social rules which past experience confirms as good.

salvation - the process of being saved by the activity (grace) of God.

sanctity of life - the specialness and uniqueness of human life based either on the will of God in creating us and sustaining us, or some rational principle as in Kantian ethics, where it is seen as inconsistent to will your own death..

secondary precept - applications by human reason of primary precepts (primary goods of natural law) to specific circumstances.

secularism - the progressive separation of private religion and public human affairs, and the evacuation of metaphysics from the realm of public debate.

sinful - sin is lawlessness, and falling short, and disobeying God.

son of god - title given to Jesus which might mean 'special anointed one' or possibly just 'the human one'.

soul - part of a human being that is metaphysical and separate from the body. Dualism is the belief we have a body and a soul and the soul goes on to eternal existence after death as a different substance. Monism argues body and soul are one.

stakeholders - all those who have an interest in the activities of a corporation, includes shareholders, employees, the local community, suppliers, the Government etc.

substance dualism - states that two sorts of substances exist: the mental and the physical. Substance dualism is a fundamentally ontological position: it states that the mental and the physical are separate substances with independent existence.

summum bonum - the greatest good, a term used in ethics for the ultimate goal or result of good actions.

superego -that part of the Freudian psyche which mediates between right and wrong and resolves conflicts between ego and id.

synderesis - a term in natural law ethics meaning we have natural innate disposition to 'do good and avid evil'. Aquinas also calls it the 'intuitive knowledge of first principles' or the primary precepts.

teleological - telos means end or purpose. So a teleological argument looks at the purpose in patterns of design in the world, as in Paley's watchmaker analogy. Teleological ethics is the ethics of purpose - as in utilitarian ethics (happiness) or situation ethics (love).

teleology - the study of purpose in nature or in ethics.

telos - Greek for purpose or end (goal)

The Forms - Plato's word for the reality behind and beyond reality which we only see as shadows in a cave. The Theory of Forms is Plato's answer to the problem "how one unchanging reality or essential being can appear in so many changing phenomena."

theodicies- rational philosophies which provide an explanation for the presence of evil in the face of the providence and goodness of God.

universalist belief - the belief that all people everywhere will eventually be saved, irrespective of their faith position.

election - the belief that God, with no regard to the will of man, made an eternal choice of certain persons to have eternal life and some to eternal damnation and that number is so fixed that it cannot be changed. Popular view in Calvinism.

utility - means 'usefulness' as in utilitarianism which states that we can make a practical calculation of happiness of the greatest number, a view made popular by Jeremy Bentham and John Stuart Mill (19th century).

verificationism - a philosophical theory that holds that for propositions to meaningful they must be susceptible to rational proof by observation.

via negativa (anaphatic way) - a philosophical approach to theology which asserts that no finite concepts or attributes can be adequately used of God, but only negative terms, such as immortal, invisible. Apophasis means 'denial, negation' and so 'apophatic' is another word for anaphatic.

via positiva (cataphatic way) - uses "positive" terminology to describe or refer to the divine – specifically, God – i.e. terminology that describes or refers to what the divine is believed to be.

vincible ignorance - ignorance that a person could remove by applying reasonable diligence in the given set of circumstances, so blameworthy ignorance, echoing Paul in Romans 2, 'the Gentiles are without excuse' because we all have the moral law written on our hearts.

whistle-blowing - the practice in business ethics whereby an employee reveals malpractice, now protected as a right in UK law.

working principles - the four principles in situation ethics which define how agape love applies in practice: personalism, positivism, pragmatism and relativism.

Postscript

Peter Baron is a UK-renowned teacher trainer and writer on Philosophy and Ethics. He read Politics, Philosophy and Economics at New College, Oxford and afterwards obtained an MLitt for a research degree in Hermeneutics at Newcastle University. He qualified as an Economics teacher in 1982, and from 2006-12 taught ethics at Wells Cathedral School in Somerset. He currently works as a freelance writer, speaker, trainer and educational consultant, and is author of revision guides, course books and study guides on the new Religious Studies specification.

In 2007 he set up a philosophy and ethics community dedicated to enlarging the teaching of philosophy in schools by applying the theory of multiple intelligences to the analysis of philosophical and ethical problems. So far over 600 schools have joined the community and over 40,000 individuals use his website every month.

To join the community please register your interest by filling in your details on the form on the website. We welcome contributions and suggestions so that our community continues to flourish and expand.

Printed in Great Britain
by Amazon

35677169R00111